MILITARY
Milionaire

How You Can Retire a Millionaire and Live a Life of Wealth (No Matter What Your Pay Grade) Using Special Military Investment Benefits and a Proven Plan for Success

CHRIS LEHTO

www.chrislehto.com

Copyright © 2016 Chris Lehto
All rights reserved.

Publishing services provided by:

ISBN-13: 978-1537305042
ISBN: 1537305042

DEDICATION AND DISCLAIMER:

This book is dedicated to the men and women of the armed services. I hope this book ignites a spark which grows into a flame. It really doesn't take a miracle to get rich, just some basic financial knowledge and a little discipline you probably learned while serving your country.

As far as financial advice, I am a fighter pilot, not a licensed financial advisor or a financial services provider. Although I believe the advice in this book and any emails I send to my subscriber list to be sound, any advice I give is simply techniques I have seen work for myself or other people. Under no condition will I accept responsibility for your climb to a million dollar net worth or your financial loss. I can't predict the future, and last time I checked, noone else can either. By downloading this book you accept responsibility for your own investment decisions. The views expressed within are my own, and in no way affiliated with the US Government. You may get a refund for the book within seven days of purchase.

THANK YOU

Thank you Claire for being an amazing wife, mother, and woman with the patience to live with me. Thank you to JP Hernandez for the idea of this book and to Casey Romijn for his extensive mortgage know-how and instruction. Special thanks to Nicole Hendrix for her uncanny editing skills, and to Kristie Ledgerwood, Joey Lott, Jon Pedlow, Tyler Derosier, Erica Ellis and Rob Archangel of the fantastic Archangel Ink team.

CONTENTS

Section 1: The Right Mentality 9

    Introduction 11

    Wealthy Is a Mindset 13

    Money Is an Idea 15

    How the Rich Get Rich and Stay Rich 19

Section 2: Building Net Worth 27

    Screw Budgeting 29

    The Magic of Compounding Interest 33

    Rule of 72: The Only Math You Need 37

Section 3: Fill the Three Pools 41

    Let the Money Flow 43

    Different Accounts for Different Purposes 49

    Filling the First Pool 53

    How to Maximize Your TSP 59

    Debt Is a Tool: Learn To Use It 67

    Start Filling the Third Pool with Cash from a Brokerage Account 75

Section 4: Real Estate 81

    Maximize the VA Loan 83

    The Three Rules of Real Estate 87

    Finding the Right Property 95

Summary – Take It One Step at a Time 101

Become a Millionaire- Start Today.. 105

References 107

About the Author 111

Section 1

THE RIGHT MENTALITY

Can't wait to start building your net worth? If so, like most military members, you probably want an *action plan*.

I've created a free downloadable action plan that will guide you on this path. It will give you simple, actionable steps you can take each day with an easy system anybody can do. No matter how busy you may be or how many times you've failed to save money in the past, with this action plan you cannot fail. Just follow the simple tasks I give you each day.

Do that, and you'll soon be watching your net worth grow. You'll have the secure knowledge that your family's financial needs are taken care of for the future. And you'll start enjoying a life of options.

You ready? Go here to get your action plan now:

chrislehto.com/actionplan

INTRODUCTION

You can be rich while still devoting your life and career to your country. While there are no legitimate get-rich-quick schemes, this book's goal is to convince you there are get-rich-slow schemes. Time is money and as long as you use your time wisely, you can become financially independent.

It will take years but it is 100% achievable. It's just math. Once you get it set up, money will start doubling all by itself. No matter what amount you start with, if you double it enough times it will become a very large number. All you need is time and a little patience. I will show you how to drop budgeting and start saving money consistently.

The government offers amazing financial benefits to those who serve their country. Whether you are in the military, state department, or civilian core, you can save an additional million dollars by simply increasing your retirement investment returns. This book will show you how to maximize your returns using the outstanding Thrift Savings Plan (TSP). It will explain everything you need to know to maximize your Veterans Affairs (VA) loan benefits. Did you know you can buy up to a fourplex with no money down? Did you know you can buy more than one property with the VA loan or that you can decrease the funding fee by thousands of dollars? Are you interested in getting a 4% interest rate on your credit card for a year? Do you want to improve your credit or learn how to fund your children's' college educations? This easy and quick read will logically explain everything you need to know to truly become financially independent.

After four years at the Air Force Academy and sixteen years in the Air Force as an F-16 fighter pilot, I have been able to grow my net worth to $650,000. As long as I can maintain a 10% growth rate on my investments (which is less than what they've already earned the past twelve years), I will reach $1M in four years, when I can retire from the military.

Introduction

Yes, I am a well-paid O-5, but there is still no excuse if you are enlisted or a lower-ranking civilian. Cory Carmichael at the Luke AFB Family Readiness Center is a retired SMSgt with a net worth over $1M, even though he didn't work any high-paying jobs after retiring from the military. He is financially independent and still working at the Family Readiness Center, teaching young airmen to start early. He used the principles in this book to save and maximize his investments. You can too. We both made mistakes along the way but still reached financial independence through a government career.

Adhering to the simple principles in this book will put you on the path to becoming a millionaire. It won't happen overnight, but it will happen. Even if you start late the best thing to do is just start. It all depends on you making the right moves and sticking to the plan. The first step is to take a few hours to read this book. The tips in this book will save you thousands of dollars in the next year and hundreds of thousands of dollars over your lifetime. Start believing it is possible because it actually is. Don't overthink it, just read the book and start acting. Good luck!

WEALTHY IS A MINDSET

In order to become wealthy, you must have the right attitude about money. You have to believe it is possible for you to be rich. Then, all you have to do is make it happen. At least you aren't holding yourself back.

I promise you can become a millionaire if you follow the basic principles in this book and have a long enough time frame. If you retire from the military, you are essentially a millionaire, already. You will get $40,000 a year in income, roughly the same amount you would receive if you had one million dollars in the bank making a modest 4% return.

The pension is already worth a million dollars even if you don't count the amazing health care benefits. All you have to do is make it to 20 years of service. Of course, this is easier said than done. Only 12% of military personnel actually make it to 20 years of service. This small percentage shows just how difficult it is to serve a full career.

If you are one of the 88% who won't make it to 20 years, or are a civilian or in the reserves, then it is even more critical you follow the guidelines in this book because you won't have a pension to fall back on. You can definitely still make it to financial independence, but you have to start early and be more aggressive.

I want to be financially independent. To me, that means I don't have to work unless I want to. In order to reach this goal, I need another million dollars in assets at retirement. Another million dollars should return an additional $40,000 a year for a combined yearly income of $80,000. At $80,000 a year in passive income, as long as my kids' colleges are paid for, I will consider myself financially independent. Even after I am financially independent, I will still work. Like everyone I know serving their country, I like to work and contribute to society. The only difference is it will be under my terms doing something I really want to do.

The simple reason you or anyone else is able to become rich is compounding interest. Albert Einstein said, "Compound interest is the eighth wonder of the world. He who understands it earns it. He who doesn't pays it." It's not difficult to understand the basic concept of compounding numbers, but our brains are just not wired to fully appreciate the power of exponential growth. The good news is you don't have to fully understand how it works to take advantage of the amazing benefits. However, you do have to internalize how important it is for your future wealth to adopt the right mentality. I will discuss compounding interest in more detail in the chapter The Magic of Compounding Interest.

If you can't easily look at your money accounts and develop plans to grow them, then the first thing you need to address is your own attitude. You simply can't get emotional about money. I do real estate as a hobby and I see people make terrible decisions all the time. They get emotional. Their "house is worth more" than the market is willing to give them. Houses are worth what people are willing to pay for them. If no one is going to pay that much for your house, then you are asking too much money. For emotional reasons, people will lose out on deals and never get to the table. They lose thousands of dollars because of some crazy idea based on feelings and emotions. Getting wealthy is a game. Nothing more. The goal is to get the highest net worth. If you make a mistake and your net worth goes down, so be it. Michael Jordan and Kobe Bryant didn't quit when they missed a shot. They shot a hundred thousand more times. You have to be in the game making deals to actually learn how the system works. You have to be prepared to fail a little to learn how to get ahead. Don't worry. As long as you prioritize growing your net worth, in the end, compound interest will ensure you are way ahead.

MONEY IS AN IDEA

Eighteen years ago my friend said, "I want my kids to grow up working so they can learn the value of a dollar." This is the working-class attitude. Work hard, make a dollar, and earn a living. That is the value of a dollar. I understand the appeal, especially after spending 20 years in a military environment. We don't want ourselves or our kids to be lazy ingrates. Working makes us tough and able to handle whatever life throws at us. Working hard to earn a living does make you appreciate what you have, but this mentality alone won't make you wealthy. I have a friend who is a Physician's Assistant. He makes over $150,000 and yet can't get a credit card because his credit is so bad. He lives paycheck to paycheck and can't get his financial life on track because "Thinking about money makes me anxious." His net worth is effectively negative. Meanwhile, as I'll show you in this book, an enlisted troop in the military who focuses on long-term wealth accumulation can get wealthy off a fraction of the income. Both the PA and the enlisted soldier work hard and contribute to society but their approach to money will produce completely opposite outcomes. Even though the PA earns a high yearly income, he blows the money on things that will not get him rich.

Although your job income does have a direct impact on how much money you can save, they are not as linked as you may believe. My PA friend, for instance, saves no money. Your lifestyle always expands to the size of your paycheck. The more you make the more things you need. How do you think people like MC Hammer go completely broke? If you have a lower income, then you are also used to a lower quality of life. You don't need a gold-plated toilet to be happy.

If you are comfortable spending $3,000 a month to live a modest lifestyle, then you don't need $3 million dollars to be financially independent. You only need $900,000 to earn the required income. If this sounds like a lot to accumulate right now, this book will show you why it isn't. How hard do you think it will be for my friend, who somehow blows $150,000 a year, to spend only $3,000 a month in retirement? He is already somehow burning $10,000 a month after taxes. In order to support this extravagant lifestyle he will need to save $3.6 million dollars. This sum is still achievable but he will have to change his mentally soon and start saving a high percentage of his income (25%). It is much easier to maintain your spending at a certain level than it is to lower it. This is why it is easier for a young enlisted troop to save more than my friend. The young enlisted troop is used to having very little money. This is a powerful weapon you should take advantage of. As the enlisted troop gains rank, if he just increases his savings with each boost in income, instead of increasing his spending, then he will save much more in the end than the PA.

The reason people such as Elon Musk, Bill Gates, and Warren Buffett can acquire billions of dollars is because dollars don't really exist. They are made up. The real truth is a dollar is just a piece of painted t-shirt. It's cotton and linen with some dye on it. The actual value of a dollar is less than 5.5 cents. You have to imagine you are dealing with monopoly money because, in reality, you are dealing with monopoly money.

Don't let your own attitude towards money freeze you into inaction. Without a doubt, money is necessary to live in the modern world, but you have to keep in mind money is just an idea. Ideas don't have boundaries. My self-proclaimed working-class friend does not want to maximize his investments because he is scared to lose money. All he wants is "a house, a truck, and a job." With his current mentality, in 20 years he will own his house and his truck, and he will have a job. In the same time frame, from the same starting point, I will have a house, a truck, and no job because I will be financially independent. Because he is scared to lose money, he is actually putting himself into a riskier situation. If he gets injured and can't work, what will his family do? They will have to make ends meet without their primary income source. Since I prioritize increasing my net worth, if something happens to me, my family will be able to live off my investments. My investments will make money so I don't have to. This is the difference between wealthy people and non-wealthy people. Financially independent people have assets working and earning money for them. As Robert Kiyosaki explains in the book *Rich Dad, Poor Dad*, don't work for money, make money work for you.

If you can change your mindset and focus on learning about money, you are guaranteed to be financially successful in life. The opposite is also true. If you don't face facts and take the time to understand the basic concepts in this book, you are guaranteed to be one of millions of Americans without wealth or savings. Many people, like my PA friend, get into a financial trap. Just thinking about money and savings makes them feel uncomfortable. Every time they look at their bank accounts they feel worried they aren't doing enough to save. So what do they do? They never look at their bank accounts. They don't take the time to figure out what they need to do to fix the problem. Since they never try and fix the problem, it never gets better and they never become wealthy. Money will make money for you by itself. All you have to do is start putting as much money as you can towards income-producing assets. Even a few dollars a day will make a huge difference over a lifetime. Compounding interest really is magic.

Here are a few other quick tips on developing the correct mentality.

The key to successful investing is taking calculated risks. The unknown is scary, but once you understand some basic principles of how money works, you will see it's not that scary. There is no need to get emotional about it. Money is just a game. We try and score the highest points.

You are going to lose money in some investments. If you don't lose money sometimes, then you are playing the game too conservatively. You have to have money to make money. Once in a while you have to lose some money to have money.

If you don't enjoy managing your investments, just diversify. Put your eggs in different investing baskets. Let time and compounding interest do its magic. If you like to manage your investments yourself, put most of your eggs in one basket, but make sure you can pull those eggs out at a moment's notice. You should also have some broken egg insurance.

Base the amount of money you put into an investment on how risky it is. Don't give all your money to your cousin for his snow cone restaurant business. But, you can give a small percentage of your net worth (.5%)—who knows, maybe the crazy kid is onto something. The risk needs to match the reward. The riskier the bet, the less money you put into it. Investors call risky bets like this "speculation" and it is basically gambling. Don't gamble with your primary investments. But you have to take calculated risks or you will never be wealthy. If you just stick your money under your pillow, or worse, spend it on frivolous things, then at least mentally prepare yourself to not be wealthy. There is no need to hide your money in your mattress.

Investing is not rocket science. Dumber and lazier people than you have made millions. You can do it. You can reach a multi-million-dollar net worth, but you have to get in the game now. You also have to be willing to learn, keep an open mind, and apply some of the discipline you learned in the military.

If you can risk everything in combat, you can risk a few made up numbers to be financially independent. A few years ago I had a business idea. I was going to leave the military to start a restaurant with a friend who already had a very successful restaurant chain overseas. He had all the restaurant know-how but did not know how to bring his product to America. I tossed the idea to some of my family. They were worried and said, "It's too risky." Meanwhile, my normal job as a fighter pilot entails real world combat.

Most military members I have met are willing to risk their life for their country, but when it comes to their bank accounts, it's too risky. People are more scared to lose their bank accounts than their lives. Yet, they will spend their money on depreciating assets. You're willing to risk going into combat, but you don't think it's worth the risk to start a new business?

If you have reservations about investing your money, try to find out why you have reservations. Is it fear of the unknown? I've found most people have deep emotional ties to money dating back to childhood. If you were brought up to "know the value of a dollar," then I challenge you to confront this idea. If a lack of knowledge is holding you back, then all you have to do is learn how money works. It is fun and exciting. Donald Trump makes one million dollars a day. All we want is a few million dollars in our lifetime. He is not smarter than you are, but he did take the calculated risks to make it happen. Once he acquired enough assets, they started making money for him and they can for you, too. First you have to understand what an asset is.

HOW THE RICH GET RICH AND STAY RICH

They build their net worth by acquiring income-producing assets. Period. This is how you get rich. You have to own things that make money. If you add up everything you own (assets) and subtract everything you owe to other people (debts), you get your net worth. In order to get rich, all you have to do is acquire as many money-producing assets as you can and minimize your debts.

When your net worth reaches a certain point, approximately two million dollars, your assets will provide enough income you will never have to work again. Do you know what your net worth is? You should. Once you start believing you can gain wealth, you have to actually start gaining wealth. How will you know if you are gaining or losing wealth if you don't even know how much wealth you have?

To increase your net worth, you have to know if what you are doing is working; you can learn that by tracking your net worth. I always know, within a few thousand dollars, what my net worth is because I use an Excel spreadsheet to track. It's not difficult or time-consuming. I spend five minutes a month logging into all my accounts and updating my assets.

In order to track your assets, first you have to know what an income-producing asset looks like. This is where people go astray and use their money in bad ways. They acquire the wrong types of assets. They spend their money on depreciating assets or assets that produce little to no income. Once you completely understand the concept of an income-producing asset, you will understand it forever. This is the most important concept in this book and the premise of *Rich Dad, Poor Dad*, an amazing finance book. The easiest way to identify an income-producing asset is to ask yourself, "Do I own it?" and "Does it make me money?" The best way to explain this is through a few examples.

Is your house an asset? Ask yourself, do you own it and does it make money for you? If, like 68% of Americans, you owe a mortgage, then you don't technically own the house.[1] Until you pay all the money back to the bank, they have a right to your house called a lien. If you don't make the payments the bank can claim ownership of the house.

But, you do own part of the house. You own the difference between how much you could sell the house for (market value) and how much you owe to the bank (mortgage). If you sell the house and pay the bank back, any money left over is yours to keep. This difference is called equity and you can use equity as leverage to do other stuff. You can borrow against it (home equity loan) or, if your house value goes up, you can refinance and get cash out of the house. The equity is an asset. It allows you to make deals and buy other stuff. Assets give you options.

Does the house make you money? As mentioned above, you can borrow against the equity. It doesn't make money but it does allow you to leverage for good or for bad. If the house appreciates in value and you sell it for a profit, then it will produce money. While you are living in it though, the house doesn't produce money. It is an asset, but it's not an income-producing asset. Home ownership is a good idea at the right time, but unless you are renting out a room of the house or using it to make money some other way, the house you live in is not an income-producing asset.

Now, let's say you are in the military or state department and have to move every three years. Instead of selling your house, you find a property manager and rent the house out as a landlord. Property managers normally charge between eight and ten percent of the monthly rent to manage your property. As long as the rent brings in more than your costs, the house has now been transformed into an income-producing asset. Ta-da! You own it, at least part of it anyway, and now it makes money for you instead of you making money for it.

In fact, if you can get positive cash flow from the rent, the house will actually pay you to own it! This is an income-producing asset. You aren't paying to own it. The asset is paying you to own it. Make sense? Donald

---

1 How Many Homeowners Have Paid Off Their Mortgages? fivethirtyeight.com/datalab/how-many-homeowners-have-paid-off-their-mortgages taken 23 March 2016

Trump can make a million dollars a day by literally doing nothing thanks to the very powerful force of positive cash flow. I count the equity in my house as an asset, but the rental houses I own are true income-producing assets. Next, let's look at an asset everyone in America, at least in the military, owns.

Is your vehicle an asset? Do you own it? Let's say you paid off your vehicle so you own that baby free and clear. Does it make money for you? Well, again, if you sell the vehicle it will make money for you, but unlike a house, which we can expect to reasonably hold value (as long as you didn't purchase it too high), a vehicle is almost always a depreciating asset. Unless you happen to drive a vintage vehicle that increases in value, your vehicle will ALWAYS lose money.

Unless you use your vehicle to produce income, it is a horrible asset. If you are an Uber driver on the weekends, then your vehicle produces income and is a depreciating income-producing asset. It will still be worth next to nothing in ten years but at least it produces something. I don't keep track of my vehicles for my net worth. To me they are necessary debts. The only thing worse than a car is a boat.

All you have to remember is "F*** the G-rides, I want the machines that are making them" (Tom Morello, Down Rodeo).[2] Buying an expensive vehicle is the single biggest mistake I see military members make. Just today I passed an E-5 driving a high-end Corvette. Unless he happens to be rich, he is giving up an amazing amount of future money to drive that car.

My friend returned from a deployment in August 2013 and bought a brand-new F-150 for $50,000 in cash. Imagine if he had bought the machines that are producing that particular G-ride, Ford stock (F). If he reinvested the dividends, which I recommend, his stock would be worth $47,000 at the time of writing.[3] The stock market decreased over that

---

2   Rage Against the Machine
en.wikipedia.org/wiki/Rage_Against_the_Machine
taken 23 March 2016

3   Stock Return Calculator with Dividend Reinvestment for Every Stock
dqydj.net/stock-return-calculator-dividend-reinvestment-drip
taken 23 March 2016

time, but his vehicle decreased a lot more. It is now worth $40,000.[4] Even in a decreasing stock market he would have made $7,000 in two years if he had not bought that vehicle.

In fact, if he wanted to keep $7,000 from a job, he would have to pay taxes on his income. In order to save $7,000 from a job he would have to actually earn $8,000. Based on his tax bracket Uncle Sam takes $1,000 of his $8,000, not to mention sales tax. A dollar saved is worth more than a dollar spent.

Let's say my friend had put that $50,000 into Apple stock instead. I bought Apple stock during that time period. At present value, March 2016, his stock would be worth $92,000. In two and a half years he would have almost doubled his money. He could now buy a brand-new F-150 and still have $42,000 left over in dividend-producing stock. As it is he has one F-150 that will go down in value several thousand dollars each year.

The simple solution is to drive a cheaper vehicle. If you want to be rich, make the sacrifice and drive a car that costs less than 10% of your net worth. Both my family's cars add up to less than 6% of our net worth. You can drive a Corvette now but you are giving up hundreds of thousands of future dollars to do so.

Is your job an asset? This is why so many business owners are rich. They do own their job. When their company earns an extra million dollars in profit, they keep an extra million dollars. For normal salaried employees like you and me, if we save the government a million dollars, we get an award and satisfaction that we saved taxpayer money, but we don't see a dime of the monetary savings.

We may not own our job, but we do own our earning potential. We can get degrees that qualify us for officer commissions or higher ranks. We can work harder and smarter than our peers to get promoted faster. Job security is relatively high in the military so we can make long-term plans

---

4   Edmunds.com

www.edmunds.com/ford/f-150/2014/for-sale/az/buckeye/?radius=50&trim=King%20Ranch&mileage=24000;38000&invtype=USED&src=clusters_1458754453406_9x2 taken 23 March 2016 based on a steady income. My salary is my primary source of income, so for right now it is my largest and most important asset by far. This is the primary asset of the middle and lower income class. If you believe you belong in the lower or middle income class, then you will most likely stay in that class. I believe I belong in the upper income class. I haven't reached the required net worth yet, but I will get there.

There are a few major problems with having job income as your primary source of money. The first and most obvious problem is you have to keep working at that job to maintain the income. What if you get injured or have a family emergency? What if you hate your job or have a personality conflict with your boss or coworkers? If it is your primary source of income, then you have few options. On the other hand, if you do your job for fun because you already have enough money to be happy, then you can leave.

The second reason job income is bad for getting rich is it's heavily taxed. If you buy a stock and then sell it more than one year later, even if you make one million dollars from the stock sale, you only pay 16.5% tax ($165,000). But, if you make one million dollars in income, based on 2014 tax laws, you pay $353,000.[5] You pay more than double the taxes if you get the money from a job versus long-term capital gains.

Capital gains is a fancy word for money coming from assets. For stocks, you have to make sure you own it for more than 365 days before you sell. For houses, you have to live in the house two out of the last five years to avoid paying taxes on any gains. When you sell your primary residence, you can make up to $250,000 in profit if you're a single owner, twice that if you're married, and not owe any capital gains taxes.[6] The key point to remember is long-term capital gains are taxed much less than regular income. The maximum taxation rate is 16.5% no matter how much money you earn.[6] Capital gains are the main reason Mitt Romney

---

5   How much would taxes be on $1 million?
www.ask.com/business-finance/much-would-taxes-1-million-b781ab5e2fdff6c4
taken 23 March 2016

6   Ten important Facts about Capital Gains and Losses
www.irs.gov/uac/Ten-Important-Facts-About-Capital-Gains-and-Losses
taken 23 March 2016

only paid 13.9% in taxes even though he made $21.6 million in 2010.[7] If you believe rich people pay their fair share of taxes, then you need to learn more about how taxes work. Rich people wrote the tax law, and they made it more favorable to make money off long-term capital income such as stocks and real estate. The tax code is unfavorable to people making the majority of their income from a job. Luckily for us, military members pay less taxes than civilians. For tracking net worth, I don't track my income as an asset, but I will definitely count my military pension as an asset if and when I actually get it.

The military pension is an amazing asset and roughly equivalent to one million dollars. If you are enlisted and can get to the rank of E-8 before you retire at 20 years, you will get approximately $30,000 in guaranteed annual income.[8] If you have one million dollars sitting in a relatively safe investment, you can expect to earn between three and five percent on your money and not lose value, equating to $30,000-$50,000 a year.

The combined income from the pension and interest on the million dollars in investments will provide you with $75,000 a year in after-tax income. Since the principal is not decreasing you can get $75,000 a year until you die. Seventy-five thousand dollars is the magic number for overall happiness according to a study done at Princeton.[9] If you retire at a higher rank, you'd need even less in additional assets to achieve this.

If you don't quite have one million dollars saved, you could still retire with less savings by spending the principal in your retirement. You run the risk of running out of money in retirement or passing nothing on to future generations, but it is definitely possible if you plan correctly and live within your means.

---

7   Why Mitt Romney and Other Wealthy Investors Pay Less Taxes
www.salary.com/why-mitt-romney-other-wealthy-investors-pay-less-taxes
taken 23 March 2016

8   Military pension calculator
militarypay.defense.gov/Calculators/ActiveDutyRetirement/High36Calculator.aspx
taken 23 March 2016

9   Do We Need $75,000 a Year to Be Happy?
content.time.com/time/magazine/article/0,9171,2019628,00.html
taken 23 March 2016

Are stocks income-producing assets? You better believe it. A stock is literally a small ownership in a company so you definitely own it. The mission of every public company is to make money for its stockholders. As long as the company is doing its job, then it is producing income and passing it into investors.

I believe stocks are one of the best ways to make money. I bought Apple stock in 2009 and sold it in 2015 for more than a 500% profit. My friend's $50,000 investment would have turned into over $275,000 in six years. Imagine making almost a quarter of a million dollars doing nothing except making a few mouse clicks. Of course, I have lost probably $30,000 in the market on other investments. It did hurt to lose that money, but it is relatively insignificant since overall, I have made over $350,000. So stocks and bonds and any instrument that buys them are income-producing assets. Without a doubt these assets should be central to your investment strategy.

What about all the other stuff we have in our houses and garages? Are these things assets? They may be things I own, but all the junk in my house and garage is pretty much just that. Junk. It will make me a small amount of money if I sell it but otherwise anything not making me money better be providing a ton of life utility or happiness because it is not going to make me rich.

Once I'm rich and my money is making money for me, I can buy whatever I want. Even if I spend some of the money coming in, my money will still be making money without me doing anything. Until my money is making a steady, adequate income stream (financially independent) then anything I buy just makes it harder to get rich.

Remember, there is always some sort of spending tax. If you buy a new truck, you will not only have to pay to register it. You will likely have to pay thousands of dollars in sales tax, both on the truck and any gas or required maintenance. Sales tax rates range from a low of 1.78% in Alaska to a high of 9.46% in Tennessee[10], accumulating to many thousands of dollars over the life of a vehicle. If you eat out a lot, not only do you pay

---

10   State and Local Sales Tax Rates in 2015
taxfoundation.org/article/state-and-local-sales-tax-rates-2015
Taken 25 June 2016

sales tax, you also have to tip another 10–20%. What if instead of buying the fancy new vehicle or eating the expensive meal, you saved the money? You would not pay an extra 9.46% in sales tax. You would effectively make that money back. It's like you just got a pay raise, but you have to save the money to get it. Although there are transaction fees on most investments, they are normally very low (or should be; don't overpay). I pay $7.99 to make any stock trade. That is less than eight dollars to sell $50,000 in stock!

Oh, but then what is money for?! "I make money so I can enjoy my life and get all the toys I want. I love my new car and my new phone and my vacations and going out and my TV and my computer and my fast internet and my fancy clothes and my kids' new bikes…"

Yeah, me too. I love all those things. Money is awesome. But in 10 or 20 or even 30 years, I will still love money and all the stuff it can do for me and my family. When I am old and can't use my body to do stuff I love, like hiking or surfing, I will still be able to afford to buy a sweet sports car, and to send my kids or grandkids to the best universities and sports camps. The key is to spend within your means today, while still saving enough for the future. Every single dollar you save today will be worth many times more in the future.

You can either buy a single $50,000 F-150 for yourself today or you can buy eight F-150s for yourself and everyone in your family in 22 years (10% interest rate compounded annually). The problem is people can't imagine they will still be around in 22 years. You or someone you love will still be around in 22 years, I promise. Would you drive an old truck if I told you I was going to give you a brand-new Lamborghini when you retire in 22 years? All you have to do is make acquiring income-producing assets a top priority. It doesn't have to be your number-one priority, but it definitely needs to be in the top five. So how do you make this happen? First, you have to start living within your paycheck.

Section 2

BUILDING NET WORTH

SCREW BUDGETING

Making and following a budget drains the fun out of life. It's terrible. Not only do I have to spend less money, I have to track what I spend? Forget it. Not doing it. You don't have to either. If you are one of the few people in this world who enjoys budgeting, then throw yourself a party because you deserve it. For the rest of us, I really don't think we need to budget. At least not down to the dollar.

The trick is using automatic payments to fill your investment accounts first, and then live off the rest. If you can't pay off your credit card bill at the end of each month, then you need to cut some recurring expenses back. On the other hand, if you have extra money left over, keep increasing your automatic payments until you can't pay off your credit card each month. Then cut expenses. Repeat this process until you can't cut anymore expenses without sacrificing quality of life. Done. Throw the *Budgeting for Dummies* book in the trash and move on.

Keep your finances simple and consistent. Autopay your investments, and then if you don't have the money at the end of the month to buy a fancy new toy, wait until the next month. Or better yet, don't buy the fancy toy. If you find you really can't live without it then cut back somewhere else.

If compounding interest is the eighth wonder of the world, then automatic payments are the ninth wonder. You won't believe how fast your net worth grows once you set up your investments on automatic contributions. The first thing you should do tomorrow (or right now if you can), is set up 10% of your paycheck to go automatically into a retirement account. Don't think twice about it. Don't say you have student loans or car payments or can't afford it. Don't make an excuse. Just go and do it. If you're in the military, I recommend the Roth TSP. Just pick an age-based option for now; you can easily change it whenever you want. I will talk later about Roth versus traditional IRA but chances are you aren't paying much in taxes right now so just go Roth. If you aren't in the military and most of your income is taxed then it probably won't matter in the long run whether you choose Roth or traditional, but I still prefer Roth.

The most important part is the money needs to go into your investment accounts before you even see it, before your lifestyle adapts to the money. By doing this one simple thing throughout your working career, even if you do nothing else for your investments, you will retire comfortably. No matter your age or your income this is the most powerful thing you can do.

It doesn't matter how much money you make, spending less than you earn will always be an issue. The more money you earn, the more things you will want to buy. Your family will want a bigger house. You will want a nicer truck. You will want to go on more expensive vacations. You will want to support your family. Money has an amazing knack for always finding a need for itself. It is so difficult for people to start saving because they are too accustomed to their current lifestyle.

The reason someone needs to budget is they are spending more money than they earn. They can't afford their lifestyle. They have to decrease the amount of money they are accustomed to spending. If you never get accustomed to spending that amount of money in the first place, you won't miss not spending it. This is the simple reason why automatic deductions from your paycheck are such a powerful investment technique. They allow you to live within your means because you are funding the important things first.

Springing for a fancy dinner is pretty tough when you have zero dollars in your bank account. However, if you've already funded your investments and have money left over, go ahead and spring for the fancy dinner once in a while. It's about consistent pressure over time. With automatic payments you are, as Kiyosaki phrases it, "paying yourself first."

As you make more money in your career, your automatic deductions will scale with your higher income. By saving a percentage of your income, each time you get a promotion, your retirement contributions will also increase. When I get a promotion, I even increase the percentage I am saving. Instead of 10%, I increase it to 11%. If you are eying a new vehicle to buy when you make your next rank, you are thinking about it backwards. This is exactly how you keep yourself from getting rich. You should be eying the new net worth number, not how you can spend your hard-earned money on some new toy. Don't get me wrong, you can still reward yourself if you earned it, but do so *after* you bump up your savings.

Like air filling a room, your lifestyle will always expand to fill your paycheck. By making the room just a little bit bigger with each promotion, you can still improve your lifestyle while prioritizing your net worth. This is the final goal. We want to enjoy our lifestyle while saving for the future.

THE MAGIC OF COMPOUNDING INTEREST

A poor horse breeder approached the richest, most feared king in the land. The horse breeder knew the king needed war steeds for his army. He offered the king a deal. Each day, he would bring his finest horse to the king. In exchange, on the first day, the king would put one grain of wheat on the first space of a chessboard. On the second day, the king would place two grains on the second space. Each day, the king would continue doubling the wheat until all the spaces were filled.

The king was happy to accept the deal and gain a fine warhorse for only a grain of wheat. However, as each day passed, the pile grew exponentially. On the final day, the king had to place a mound of wheat larger than Mount Everest. In a little over two months, compounding interest grew a single grain into 1,000 times the entire global production of wheat in 2010![11]

The king had the horse breeder executed and took all the wheat back. The moral of the story is don't be a greedy horse breeder. You don't need to double your money every day to be rich. But you do need to get as high an interest rate as possible at the lowest risk. You want double digit percentages or at least high single digits.

Just like you don't need to know how electricity works to use a light switch, you don't need to understand how interest rates work to take advantage of them. It is all about what kind of return you can get on your money. Consistently getting 15% annual return on the money you invest, no matter how much you start with, will get you rich. Every time the money doubles, it is increasing as much in that single doubling period as it increased all of the time before combined. Imagine you have been saving for fifty years and have five million dollars. If you get 15% in interest that

---

11   Wheat and chessboard problem
en.wikipedia.org/wiki/Wheat_and_chessboard_problem
taken 30 March 2016

The Magic of Compounding Interest

money will double to ten million dollars in 4.8 years (I calculated this using the Rule of 72, which I will explain in the next chapter.) You made more money in the last five years than you did in the previous fifty. In another five years it will increase ten million dollars, increasing more in those final five years than it did in the entire fifty-five years prior. As long as you get a high enough interest rate, it is just a matter of time before you have millions of dollars.

This is why interest rates matter. If you invest $1000 for your kid when he is born and add nothing else ever again, your son will retire at age 65 with $490,000 (based on the average long-term stock return of the market, 10%). Let's say you can get a remarkable 15% return on your money. Now your son will retire with $8.8 million! You read that correctly: almost nine million dollars from only $1000.

That is the magic of compounding interest. It is all about the percentage rate. You have to maximize the percentage return you get from your assets while minimizing the interest percentage you pay on your debts. This is the primary difference between the wealthy and the working class. The working-class mentality is to minimize debt. The wealthy mentality is to minimize interest rate on debts, and maximize interest rate on assets. Donald Trump has billions of dollars in debt, but he still somehow makes one million dollars a day.

Fifteen percent is a remarkable return on investment but it is definitely possible. From 1979–2011, Warren Buffet averaged a 19% annual return on investment.[12] At this rate your son would retire with $82 million dollars. So maybe you aren't Warren Buffett (you could be; he is human after all), but what if you could get just one more percentage point, 11%? At an 11% return, your son would retire with $890,000. A small increase in the rate of return almost doubled your money.

A friend asked me if she should put her three-year old daughter into private preschool. What if instead of paying $15,000 for one year's private school tuition she put the money into her daughter's Roth retirement account? Based on average historical returns, her daughter would have

---

12 Chasing Warren Buffett's Alpha
blogs.cfainstitute.org/investor/2012/09/11/chasing-warren-buffett-alpha
taken 2 April 2016

$5.5 million dollars when she is 65. Her daughter wouldn't have to save a single dime in her life and she would still retire a multi-millionaire. You can't technically open a retirement account for your child when they are three years old but you can save for college.

Sending her daughter to free public school and instead putting that $15,000 into a tax-advantaged college savings account, a 529 plan, will return $62,600 15 years later at 10% interest. The cost of one year of private preschool would pay for one year of tuition, room, board, and fees at Harvard.[13]

She can send her kid to private preschool or arguably the best university in the world for the same amount of money. It's not the same amount of money now, but it is in 15 years, assuming 10% interest. If she can get 15% then she will have $122,000 and can pay for two years at Harvard.

Each interest point counts. People spend days shopping for a new TV or a new phone. They research every little detail about a new vehicle. They spend countless hours reading blogs, vehicle specs, pricing options. They read books on how to negotiate with the dealer, the best time of year to buy, and which model gives the best value. But when it comes to a car loan for the vehicle, they just call their bank and accept the rate. This is insanity. They don't even ask for a lower rate.

Here is another thing the wealthy know. EVERYTHING is negotiable. Especially when the price tag is bigger. It is worth the seller's time to put the price high. If you don't negotiate and accept the high price, they just made thousands of dollars. If you do negotiate, they can use their skill and experience to make sure you pay the maximum amount you are willing to pay. Loans are worth a lot of money. It is worth it to the seller to just put a higher rate on the initial loan quote.

When you buy a home, do you get more than one quote for the mortgage? Chances are good that you don't. You probably spend weeks, maybe months, picking out the right house. But when it comes to the mortgage loan, I bet you don't spend more than a few minutes. Did you ask for a

---

13   Harvard at a Glance
www.harvard.edu/about-harvard/harvard-glance
taken 2 April 2016

lower rate? The first mortgage quote I got on my current house was 4.0%. I spent a few hours and got ten other quotes. It was easy. I used Lending Tree and mortgage people started calling me. They tried to keep me on the phone answering questions for them, but I just said, "My credit is over 750. What is your annual percentage rate (APR) and funding fee for a VA loan up to $415,000?" If they didn't immediately answer or if they paused to find the answer, then I kindly told them I had to go and thanked them for their time. My first quote after starting the Lending Tree process was 3.25% with $1,000 back at closing. Once I got a 3.25% interest rate quote my question became "Can you beat 3.25% APR and $1,000 back at closing?"

It took me about an hour of actual work to save tens of thousands of dollars. The original guy who quoted me 4.0% came back with 3.25% but no money back at closing. I told him I was getting 3.25% and $1,000 back at closing. I think he was actually crying on the phone when I told him his deal wasn't good enough. I laughed after I hung up. Business is business. If they can't match the deal, they can't match the deal. You don't owe these people anything. Every one of the brokers calling you for a VA loan will be ex-military and they will let you know this fact right away. It is their job to make the most money for their company or themselves. The only regret you should feel is regret they couldn't get you a better deal. You don't have to be mean about it. Be honest and nicely tell them you have a better offer so you are going to take it. Thank them for their time, and tell them to call you if they can make a better deal.

RULE OF 72: THE ONLY MATH YOU NEED

72/interest rate = years to double.

The Rule of 72 is a quick way to figure out how fast your money will double for each specific interest rate. Divide the interest rate into 72, and you will find how many years it takes for your money to double. If you are getting the historical average of the stock market, 10%, it will take 7.2 years for your money to double (72/10=7.2). If you have $1,000 and are going to retire in 21 years, at 10% interest your money will double three times. $1000 to $2,000 to $4,000 to $8,000. When you retire your $1,000 will have turned into $8,000. If you retire in 28 years it will be $16,000, and at 35 years your $1,000 investment will be $32,000.

If you are only getting 7% on your money because you pay some mutual fund manager 1.5% and he picks safer assets, then it will take 10 years for your money to double. 72/7=10.28. In the same 35-year period, instead of it doubling 5 times to become $32,000, your $1,000 investment only doubles 3.5 times to become $12,000. A measly 3% difference in your rate of return cut your final amount by almost two-thirds. This is why minimizing fees is so important. The TSP is currently a great investment vehicle because the fees are so low. They really do have a world-class retirement fund and you should take advantage of it.

The Rule of 72 highlights the power of compounding interest. Even if you only get 7% on your investments, you will still have twelve times your investment after 35 years. Instead of buying one F-150, now you can buy twelve of them in 35 years at 7%, or 32 F-150s at 10% interest rate. Instead of one F-150 now you can have $1.6 million dollars in 35 years. You have to make sure you aren't paying a bunch of worthless fees to other people.

The Rule of 72 is a great motivational tool. It quickly reminds me how much saving can pay off. Right now, I really want an automated pool pump for my pool. Is $1,500 automated pool pump really worth $48,000 in my retirement? Right now you may think 35 years is a long time. And it is. But, I bet you know a 73 year old still able to do fun and exciting things.

People are living longer and longer. By taking care of yourself and staying in shape, you can easily live into your 90s and maybe over 100 years old. Somehow we think we won't use or like money in the future, but I will want to travel and visit my grandkids when I am old and $48,000 buys a lot of plane tickets.

Start working the Rule of 72 into your investment accounts. Even if you only have a few thousand dollars, it is fun and motivating to think of what your savings will turn into. At a completely realistic 10% rate of return, in 35 years $3,000 will turn into $96,000! You literally don't have to do any work for $93,000. All you have to do is not spend the saved money and make sure it is getting the historical average of the stock market. And that is only $3,000. Let's say you can buckle down this year and save $10,000. That will turn into $320,000! If you get a $15,000 bonus, that money will be $480,000! Imagine, all you have to do is not spend the bonus on frivolous stuff which is going to break anyway and you will make $465,000. This is a lot of money for not doing anything, and is completely possible. Do it two years in a row, and now you have almost $1 million. You don't even have to save anymore after that if you don't want to.

I have stopped contributing to my retirement accounts. Screech, the music stops. Sound crazy? Not at all. I used the Rule of 72 and found I will have more than enough money when I am 59 1/2 years old and can start to withdraw from my retirement accounts. I can withdraw before that age but I will have to pay a 10% penalty. In 21 years, when I am 59 1/2 years old, at 10% rate of return I will have $3.6 million dollars, just from my retirement stocks, not including my real estate investments or my military pension. That is enough money for what I think I am going to do.

I am not saving for retirement, but I am still saving. I'm not accustomed to living on the money so it was easy to divert it to a different saving vehicle. I put the money into my children's 529 college savings plan.

Which brings us to what to save for. I am no longer saving for retirement, so what should I save for next?

Section 3
FILL THE THREE POOLS

LET THE MONEY FLOW

A good analogy for money is water. You may have heard of different income streams. I currently have a few different income streams. My primary income is my salary from the military and it is a river. Each of my two rental properties are small streams feeding into the river. My hobbies on the side, being a realtor and an author, are even smaller streams which sometimes go the opposite direction and actually take money from the river.

Any useless debt you take on, however is taking from your income river and not providing any long-term benefit. An expensive vehicle or boat will take a large amount from the river. Consistent and automatic payments make a difference, so focus on decreasing the streams leaving your river and increasing all the tributaries adding to it.

If money is water, then think of different savings vehicles as pools. The old adage is buckets but I think buckets are too small. I don't want buckets of money, I want pools. Imagine you are at the end of your income river spending all the money coming into your hands. If you are like me, you spend all the money you get.

That is why the savings pools are placed upstream from you and me. They divert some of the river before we even see the money. The diverted water flows through a canal into a series of vats. Money doesn't leave these pools. It only pours in and grows until enough time has passed. It's like aging barrels of wine. We are turning our small amount of water into expensive wine and it takes years. In the end, it will be worth it.

Imagine three pools in a row. The idea is to fill the pools up in order of priority. The first pool is long-term retirement, the second pool is the kids' college, and the third pool is current wealth. If you don't have kids then you can just skip the second pool and go right to current wealth accumulation. Until the first pool fills up, I am always contributing something to it. The first pool is the most important pool by far. The second pool is also important but it is pretty small. We focus on the third pool after the first two are funded. Funded means I don't need to add anymore because I have reached my savings goals. For instance, I don't contribute to my retirement accounts because they are funded. I will contribute my last amount to my children's 529 this year. After that, all of my savings will go towards current wealth.

If you read any other finance book they will say the first pool you fill should be an emergency fund where you save six months of your spending. This is a good idea to write down in a book but to me it seems like a waste of money, especially if you are in the military. First of all, we already have very good job security. If I leave the military before my commitment is up, I will go to jail. That is pretty high job security. If something terrible happens and I die or am injured, I have life insurance and healthcare insurance. The government does a good job of taking care of us and our families.

The second reason I don't need a dedicated emergency fund is I have assets to fall back on because I have been saving in my investment accounts. If I need cash, I can sell some stock from my brokerage account and have the cash in three days. If I need the money in less than three days, then I can use my credit cards and just pay the credit card back with stock sales.

You don't need an emergency fund, but you do need access to some short-term money in case something happens. If you are using the TSP (which you should be using if you've gotten this far in the book), you can take out up to $50,000 of your TSP and pay it back later. There are some restrictions. I don't recommend ever taking from your retirement accounts, but if it is a real emergency you can break the TSP glass. You can research this option more at the tsp.gov site.

The best type of income pool is the type filling itself up. Stocks and, especially, low-fee index funds, such as the ones offered in the Thrift Savings Plan, are a fantastic way to start filling up your retirement pool. This should be the first pool you fill. If you have high-interest debt, such as credit card debt, you should be focusing your effort on driving that debt to zero, but you should still be investing towards your long-term pool.

For military members or federal employees their first priority should be the TSP. If you don't have access to the TSP then prioritize your company's 401(k). If neither is an option, then I recommend you contribute to an IRA at Vanguard or another low-cost index provider.

Go for 10% of your base salary. You can do it. And then do whatever you have to do to lower your credit card debt. Don't get emotional about it, make it a game. If you spend too much money on food, eat at the base chow hall. I'm an O-5 and I eat at the base chow hall. It's the healthiest food I can find on and around base and it is by far the cheapest. The air-traffic controllers I work with order out almost every night. If they ate at the base eating facility, how much money would they save a month? $100? $200? Even $100 a month will pay off a credit card quickly or fund an IRA.

The government operated Thrift Savings Plan (TSP) is an amazing investment vehicle. It has low management fees and tracks the major indexes. Instead of a person choosing particular stocks, a computer buys a small amount of each stock in a broad category or index. One of the supposed disadvantages of the TSP is its lack of options. Personally I think this is an advantage. I will talk in more detail about TSP funds in the chapter How to Maximize Your TSP.

Once your first pool has a decent amount of money, say $30,000, then you should focus on the next largest cost. If you are a civilian, I recommend your second pool be saving for a down payment for your house. Those of you with VA loan eligibility will be able to get a loan allowing you to buy a house with no money down, so you won't have to save for this. To see how big a deal this is, imagine instead of putting $50,000 down on a house, you can put that same money into your TSP. Use the Rule of 72 to figure out how much money you will have when you retire. It is a large number. For folks who can get a VA loan, your second largest cost in life will be college tuition.

How much do you need for college? I recommend $80,000 at the time of college entrance for each kid. In today's money the average public university costs $24,000 a year, so $80k will cover 80% of the costs for four years.[14] I am going to stress scholarships and tuition assistance to my kids. If they can't pay for at least part of their college with sports or academic scholarships, then they can work part time while they are at school. If they don't go to college, I can just give them the money, but I will likely pay normal taxes when I take it out of the college savings vehicle.

The government grants an amazing benefit to military personnel to help with this: the Post-9/11 GI Bill benefits transfer. If you can, you should without a doubt transfer benefits to your kids. I am still amazed Congress passed this benefit. It's almost as if they don't know the power of compounding interest because they will pay for one child's entire college education decades in the future. The first GI bill educated our WW2 veterans and resulted in amazing growth and prosperity for America. This benefit is worth about $80,000 in today's money.

If I can supplement enough, hopefully my kids won't have to take out loans for their education. Two-thirds of students graduating from American colleges are graduating with some level of debt. The average debt is $26,600.[15] This is a lot of debt to start out adult life with. Too many young adults these days go into huge debt paying for a university degree. Unless they are in a high-paying field such as medicine or law, it can be stressful and difficult for them to pay it back.

My goal by saving for my kids' education is to provide enough financial benefit to minimize this stress. If they do get into an amazing private university, I will not pay the full price. It just isn't worth it. I would rather put that money in a retirement account for them. Putting one year of costs at Harvard into a retirement account for them allows them to retire with $6.1 million, without saving another dime. Seriously. Would you rather get to say "my child is at Harvard" for one year or give them a $6 million gift they can live on until they die?

---

14 What's the Price Tag for a College Education?
www.collegedata.com/cs/content/content_payarticle_tmpl.jhtml?articleId=10064
taken 8 April 2016

15 How the $1.2 Trillion College Debt Crisis is Crippling Students, Parents and the Economy
www.forbes.com/sites/specialfeatures/2013/08/07/how-the-college-debt-is-crippling-students-parents-and-the-economy/#481a637d1a41
taken 9 April 2016

Long story short, I plan for $80,000 per kid. I think college education is extremely important, but it is simply one more thing in life. It is not the only thing in life and $80k is still a lot of savings. Don't sacrifice your own retirement so your kids can go to a better school. It's just not worth it. There are decent public schools out there or you can get financial aid, scholarships, or grants.

To save $80K, use the Rule of 72 backwards to figure out how much you need to save now. I have three kids. My first kid will use the GI bill so she is done. The next kids are currently four and two. My four-year-old has 14 years until she starts college, and my two-year-old has 16 years. I won't need all the money right at the beginning so let's make it 16 years until I need the money. If I can get 10% interest the money doubles every 7 years. So if we go backwards 2.3 doubling periods, I will learn how much I need to save now (16 years until college/7 years to double = 2.3 doubling periods). If I halve $160,000 2.3 times I get $32,500 ($160,000 to $80,000 to $40,000 to 32,500). I need a total of $32,500 in money saved now for two kids. So if you have one kid who is 2 years old, you need $16,250 saved in a well managed 529. If you put $350 a month into a 529 right when the child is born, you can stop contributing after three years and you will reach this savings goal. If you start saving later then you will have to save more money over a longer period of time.

I will go into further detail later, but I recommend a low-cost 529 plan. A 529 plan, named after the 529 section of the IRS tax code, is basically a Roth retirement account but for college savings.

The third and final pool should be current assets and income. This pool is filled with unsheltered money in brokerage accounts, businesses, and rental properties. Once this pool is overflowing, I will use the excess money to live. This is the money I can use to buy a Ferrari if I want. I would love to own a Ferrari, but I can't bring myself to do it because it is such a waste. Instead I will use the money to buy other assets. The third pool is financial independence. It's only possible to fill this pool once I have filled up the two most important pools: my retirement and my kids' college fund. After all, what else do I need to pay for in the future besides my own living expenses? Nothing.

DIFFERENT ACCOUNTS FOR DIFFERENT PURPOSES

Before we begin talking about how to fill your pools, let's review the different types of accounts you can use to accomplish this. The big accounts you need a general understanding of (because you should own them) are the traditional Individual Retirement Account (IRA), the Roth IRA, the 401(k)/TSP, the 529, and the brokerage account.

These accounts are just folders you put assets in. The assets can be whatever type of equity you want. Assets can be cash, stocks, bonds, real estate investment trusts, or funds owning those things like index funds and mutual funds. The assets can even be real estate but this is rare. Think of cash or pieces of stock paper sitting in each folder.

Another point of confusion is what mutual funds and index funds are. A fund is just a group of equities picked by a person or a software program. These vehicles are like mixed nuts bags at the super market. You could buy different nuts and combine them in bags but it is a lot easier to just buy the mixed nuts bag. The pistachios and peanuts are already shelled, which is convenient, but the costs are going to be higher. You can even put houses and other assets into retirement accounts. Mitt Romney has one of these in the Cayman Islands. It is pretty rare and only a few dozen banks have self-directed IRAs that allow real estate but it's possible.

You just assign these assets into a folder. Unless you are in a specific company or government plan like the TSP or 401(k), you can move money from one bank to another and from one folder to another. For instance, my wife moved her Roth IRA from Bridgeway to Vanguard last month and I am in the process of moving our 529 college savings from USAA to Vanguard because the rates are lower. As long as the new folder is the same type as the old folder, there is no problem.

Different Accounts for Different Purposes

We put assets into certain folders so the government knows what tax advantages to give us. The government wants us to save for our retirement and our children's education, so it gives tax advantages to money we put away long term. It is a great benefit our country provides us, but you have to use the money for its intended purpose, retirement or college. You can still remove the money at any time but you will pay a penalty (usually 10%).

A traditional IRA is a retirement fund where any money you put into that folder is not taxed. Instead, the money is taxed when you take it out. If you put $10,000 into your traditional TSP account, and you're in the 15% tax bracket, the government will give you $1,500 back at tax time. The TSP automatically does this for you so you don't have to do anything. They make it so easy it is ridiculous. When you take that money out when you are 59 ½ years old, you will have to pay taxes on it. So if $10,000 turned into $160,000 28 years later, assuming you are in the same tax bracket, you will have to pay 15% of 160K which is $24,000. In the end your $10k turned into $136K ($160K minus $24K). This is how a traditional IRA works. You get a tax benefit putting the money in, but are taxed when you take it out. It still is a great advantage.

The Roth IRA is the reverse of the traditional IRA. The money is taxed when you put it in but tax-free when you take it out. The argument for a Roth IRA is you save money because the compounding interest gains are not taxed. So on the same $10,000 savings you set aside, $1,500 goes to Uncle Sam. You actually start with $8,500. At 10%, 28 years later this increases to $136K (calculated using the Rule of 72). The exact same amount as the traditional IRA! Why? We started with more money in the traditional IRA, so why didn't compounding interest leave us with more in the end? Because the tax rate going in was the same as the tax rate going out. The compounding interest argument only works if you think you will be paying a higher tax later than you are now. Military members are taxed at a lower rate than civilians, but when we retire, our income is looked at the same as normal civilian income. We will likely pay higher taxes later as civilians than when we are in the military. It makes more sense to pay the taxes now and avoid any future uncertainty, so a Roth IRA is more logical.

Also, the great thing about a Roth IRA is you don't have to worry about what the government does to the tax rate in the future. I can't imagine they will lower taxes. The first George Bush said, "Read my lips, no new taxes," and even he raised taxes. Not only will we most likely pay more taxes as civilians, in all likelihood the government will be forced to raise taxes because of overspending. A Roth IRA protects against both instances, so choose Roth. If you are a civilian already paying high taxes and you think there is a chance you will pay lower taxes in retirement, then a traditional IRA is probably a better option.

The next account type, the 401(k), is named after section 401(k) of the IRS tax code. 401(k) programs are retirement pension vehicles companies are allowed to provide for employees. The TSP is designed to resemble the 401(k) and Roth 401(k) plans. These programs follow the traditional or Roth IRA rules, but have a higher contribution limit. As of 2016, you can only contribute a total of $5,500 per year to a traditional or Roth IRA, but you can contribute $18,000 per year to your TSP or 401(k) plan. If you deploy to a combat zone you can contribute up to $53,000 and that money can be tax-exempt. Remember the F-150? There are also income limits to a Roth IRA, while your TSP has no income limits.

The 529 college savings account is very similar to a Roth IRA, but it has to be used for college and each account is state run. It's called a 529 because the rules are under IRS section 529. As long as the state allows, and most do, you can save in any state and use the money in another state. So it doesn't matter where your kids go to school. You can live in California, invest in a Nevada plan, and send your kids to a college in Texas. Disregard the state and look at the plan. Make sure the plan allows the money to be used in any state.

I signed up initially with USAA's Nevada 529 plan because it was easy but switched to Vanguard because USAA's plan, like most plans, has very high management fees. Financial analysts at USAA are paying their salaries with my kids' college money. By the way, they get a lower return than a computer-bought index fund. The difference in costs is dramatic.

Make sure you check the fees before picking a plan. If they are hiding the price it's for a reason. It's like buying food at a restaurant where there are no prices on the menu. The only people truly looking out for you and your

Different Accounts for Different Purposes

financial welfare are you and your family, so do your due diligence. I love USAA. They are a great bank and insurer. But for all their advertising, USAA is a bank. Whatever their employees think, banks exist for the sole purpose of making money.

To find fees for 529 plans and compare plans, I recommend www.savingforcollege.com. They compare each 529 plan and tell you how much they cost. The Vanguard 529 plan costs a total of 0.19% a year. Although the USAA 529 plan costs only 0.15% a year in fees to USAA, the mutual funds they choose charge another 0.54-0.99% for a total minimum fee of 0.65%. To add insult to injury, those extra fees get you less return on your investment.

The USAA 529 plan is not the worst and saving anything is better than saving nothing, but I recommend spending a few minutes to research your different options. Even a 0.5% difference will mean many thousands of dollars over time. SavingforCollege.com has several 5-star rated plans you can use.

The Coverdell education savings account (ESA) is another option if you need to pay for private K-12 education. Unfortunately, it has a $2,000 limit on annual contributions and as I showed earlier, paying for education the government provides for free is a terrible investment. But, if you have to send your kids to private high school, then the Coverdell ESA will give you the same tax benefits as a 529.

The last account to know about is the brokerage account. A brokerage account is just an account you can use to trade stocks (or index funds or mutual funds). Think of a brokerage account as an unshielded account. An IRA is shielded or sheltered from paying some taxes. A brokerage account is not, so if you buy and sell any sort of company equity (stock, bond, index fund, mutual fund) inside a year, the government will see it as normal income. That money goes into your normal income folder for your taxes. If you wait over a year to sell the equity, then it goes into a different folder, the capital gains folder, and it is taxed less (up to a max of 16.5%). The brokerage account should be the primary account you use to build current wealth. I will discuss brokerage accounts in depth in a later chapter.

FILLING THE FIRST POOL

Investing in the stock market through the TSP or by buying individual stocks in an IRA is the easiest and simplest way to increase wealth. I also like real estate as an investment vehicle, but houses can't keep doubling in price like stocks can. If they did, in a few generations there wouldn't be enough money in the world to pay for a place to live. A single piece of real estate could theoretically keep increasing in value but even in New York, where real estate prices are astronomical, houses still have to be affordable to someone. There are countless examples of small company stocks doubling many, many times.

A second benefit of using stocks as your primary investment vehicle is stocks are liquid. You can make money in real estate, but it is more complicated and requires more than just clicking a few buttons on a website. Liquidity is how fast you can access your money. For an emergency fund you need access to cash quickly. If all your money is tied up in your house because you want to be debt-free, you will have to sell your house or get a new loan from the bank in order to access your equity. On the other hand, in three days I can sell my stocks and get thousands of dollars in cash. If some amazing business opportunity comes along I can pounce on it. If there is another housing crash, guess who has the cash to start buying houses from the banks? Rich people have cash available in order to take advantage of opportunities.

In Phoenix, after the 2008 housing crash, you could have thrown a dart at a map and find great properties for sale at half their value. People couldn't sell houses fast enough. Banks wouldn't lend money so there were no buyers. If you had cash, you were suddenly king. You know who doesn't need a bank loan? Rich people. How many houses could you have bought during the housing crash with a few hundred thousand dollars? Having money liquid and available cannot be underestimated.

Even if you put your money in a retirement account such as the TSP to gain tax benefits, you can still borrow against it. I guarantee you could have bought a decent, livable house for $50,000 in Phoenix in 2008, the amount you can take out of the TSP. Rich people have cash because they know what cash can do. Working-class people have a house and a job to make cash to live on. Rich people save cash so it can make them more cash.

Investing in stocks, like everything else in life, is about timing. If you had bought $1,000 of Netflix a few months after its initial offering, when it was priced at 47 cents, and sold in April 2016, that small investment would be worth $215,000. Of course, finding a stock like that at the right time is difficult. It's easy to find Netflix stock now. Just look at any article on stock investing and I bet they mention it. But, back when Netflix first went public and started selling shares they were difficult to find. There are always opportunities but there are many fewer opportunities when the market is priced very high overall.

In January 2009, I was looking heavily into stocks. I picked Google, Netflix, and Apple. They were in industries I liked and understood. They all had great products, good management teams, and good balance sheets. They all did well. It was like buying a house in 2008 in Phoenix. In 2008 if I had just thrown a dart at any list of the top ten technology stocks, I would have picked a winner. That's pretty much what I did. Everyone around me was crying about how the market had crushed their investments and I was ecstatic. Here was an amazing opportunity. I invested all the cash I could come up with, $20,000. Then I sold my stake in Google and Netflix and put all my cash into Apple. Apple did the worst out of those stocks and still increased five-fold. I made over $100,000 in six years. Not a bad way to earn $100K. I literally just clicked a few buttons and then watched it go up in value for six years. I've made money off houses but not that kind of money and it was way more difficult. Unfortunately, you have little chance of doing this in an overpriced market. The prices of stocks are simply too high. They are overpriced.

How do you know if a stock is priced high or low? To know the actual value of a stock, you can't just look at the price. The price means nothing on its own because the company can just sell more pieces of stock. It's like saying my car costs $20,000 without saying what kind of car it is. If it's a

Ferrari, then you better check if it's drivable because that is unbelievably cheap. But if it's a used Honda Civic with 250,000 miles then $20,000 is way too high.

You have to look at the price of each piece of stock based on how much money each piece of stock makes. An easy ratio to figure this out is the powerful price over earnings ratio, or P/E. The P/E for a stock is like the blue book value of a car. A stock with a higher P/E is generally riskier. In order to get a return on your money, the company has to grow its earnings faster. The best way to use P/E is to compare the P/E of the stock you are interested in to other stocks in its industry. For example, you can compare the P/E for Apple with that of IBM. They aren't necessarily direct competitors but they are both large brand-name computer companies.

Apple's P/E is 11.88 and IBM's is 11.17. Look up any stock on the internet and the P/E will already be calculated for you. Based on P/E, IBM and Apple are roughly the same price. Which would you choose? A good technique is to imagine it is a job interview. Where will each company be in two, four, and ten years? Personally I believe Apple has a better chance to increase its profits in the future so I would choose Apple over IBM.

IBM has a higher dividend yield. If you wanted to retire and needed income, a higher dividend yield may make IBM a better deal. What's a dividend? A public company's primary job is to make money for its shareholders. If the company is making a ton of money, then they may choose to return some of the profits back to the shareholders as cash dividends.

IBM's dividend is currently 3.42%, and Apple's dividend is 1.87%. By buying $100 worth of each stock, each year IBM will give you $3.42 and Apple will give you $1.87. If you take the dividends into account, IBM is a little cheaper than Apple and, based on what your goals are, IBM may be a better investment at the current price. Dividends are important and can allow you to live off your stock investments without having to sell the stock. Also remember most dividends are taxed at the lower capital gains rate.

Each industry is different though, so remember to compare similar companies. Utility companies and household consumables are notoriously low P/E industries. You will probably keep buying the same washing machine detergent for years. It is a very competitive market dominated by a few stalwarts. Biotechnology on the other hand is known for having very high P/E ratios. If a new genetic trait hits it big then it has huge return on investment and the company is an amazing success, but most fail so it is a very risky business.

Since the ratio is different for each industry you can't really use it to compare across industries. You want to compare apples to apples. Think of it as price/square foot for houses. Each neighborhood is like a separate industry. You wouldn't compare a New York apartment to a farmhouse in Montana. You would compare a New York apartment to one right across the street.

Let's use the P/E to compare Apple with Netflix. As of writing, Apple's P/E is 11.88. Netflix's is 373.2! The P/E ratio means if you buy a piece of Apple stock, it will take 11.88 years for that stock to pay you back based on their current earnings. If you give your cousin $100 for his lemonade stand, it will take him 11.88 years to pay you back if his business has a P/E of 11.88. But at current income, it will take Netflix 373.2 years to pay you back! This means Netflix investors believe Netflix's earnings will greatly increase in the future. If the company's earnings go up, each piece of stock earns a little more money and it takes less time to pay the investors back. The P/E gets lower because the E goes up. The denominator gets bigger.

I believe investors in Netflix are taking a huge risk. This is what it means when people say the growth is "priced into the stock." To make the amount of money priced into Netflix's stock price, they need exponential growth in earnings. Netflix has great growth, but it is not exponential. I personally do not see how Netflix could grow to make that much money. And even if it is possible, what if something happens along the way? What if a Chinese competitor opens in China? What if the Chinese government doesn't allow Netflix to operate in China? What about India? They do have their own great content but it's not like online streaming can't be copied. For me, there are simply way too many risk factors associated with Netflix at that price. If the P/E was 30, like its industry average, then it is a fantastic investment. But at 373.2 it is very highly priced. There is a chance it will miraculously explode into a worldwide content company, but is it worth the risk?

This is how you use P/E to get a simple big-picture overview of how expensive a stock is. You don't have to be a stock master to apply some basic common sense.

HOW TO MAXIMIZE YOUR TSP

You don't have to be a stock genius to take advantage of the market. Index funds, such as what the TSP uses, are amazing vehicles. I do believe you can maximize your returns if you use a little stock market know-how. There are a few very basic game plans you can employ to maximize your stock market returns.

Keep it simple at the beginning. Focus on setting up automatic payments to start building your nest egg. Then, over the years you can learn more and try to maximize your investments. The TSP is just a military version of a 401(k). It is a tax-advantaged retirement account. You can do both traditional (taxed later when you take it out, not now) or a Roth (taxed now, not when you take it out).

The TSP has five funds: the G, F, C, S, and I funds. The G fund is what your money defaults into when you sign up for the TSP. It is US government treasuries and basically cash. It only gets 2–3% a year so if you haven't updated your allocations you won't have lost much but I can guarantee you won't have made much money either. At 2.5% interest it will take 28.8 years for your money to double (72/2.5=28.8.) I have all of my TSP money in the G fund currently because I suspect the market will go down.

The other funds are designed to replicate certain indexes, which is why they are called index funds. The C fund replicates the Standard and Poor 500. This index is made up of 500 large – to mid – capitalization companies and is a great overall stock market tracker. The S fund is the most aggressive index and replicates small US companies. The I fund tracks international companies and the F fund replicates a broad US bond index.

These funds are passively managed by a computer. For this reason, index funds have very low fees. According to a study released June 2015 by Morningstar, actively managed funds lagged their passive counterparts across nearly all asset classes, especially over a ten-year period from 2004 to 2014. Passive index funds purchasing a little bit of everything, did better than professional stock pickers. Compared to actively managed mutual funds, the passive computer approach is more effective for long-term investing. The one exception I have seen is for income investing. If you want a steady stream of dividends and income, then there are some excellent hedge funds available, but most have high entry investment requirements.

The TSP also has managed funds, called L funds, which select a different allocation of the five funds based on when you will retire. The L funds are good for a set-it-and-forget-it approach to stock investing. Overall, it is hard to beat the TSP as a retirement investment vehicle, but don't overthink it. Put in at least 10% of your base salary. We will talk later about which fund to choose but it is easy to change so for now just get it going.

Roth versus Traditional—Think of an IRA like a folder. The government grants anything inside this folder tax advantages. What most people don't know is you can move these folders around. I have a Roth IRA I started at USAA. I use this fund to buy and sell stock because I don't have to report anything I do inside a Roth IRA to the government. The money I make inside this folder is tax-free. If I take this money out before I am 59 ½ years old, I will pay a penalty. As long as I wait until after that age, I don't have to pay any taxes on the money.

The negative to a Roth IRA is I have to put in money that is already taxed. The other type of IRA, called a traditional IRA, is the opposite. You don't pay taxes on the money when you put it in, but when you take it out you have to pay taxes on it. If you are a civilian, it doesn't make that big a difference if you choose Roth or traditional, according to the math I have done. But since military members pay much lower taxes while we are in the military, a Roth IRA is the better way to go. A large portion of my pay is not taxed. In 2015, being in the military saved me $10,000 in taxes[16], and I didn't even enter any combat zones. If I had deployed to a combat zone the number saved in taxes would be higher.

---

16   What is your tax bracket?
www.bankrate.com/calculators/tax-planning/quick-tax-rate-calculator.aspx

When we separate or retire from the military, our tax burden will increase substantially. This is why a Roth IRA is a better option for military members, and why I am so happy they added the feature to the TSP. We are paying less in taxes now than we probably will in the future since the military grants us tax benefits. No one can predict how much taxes will lower or rise in the future but based on our country's current debt level, I'm pretty sure they won't be lower. So bottom line, start adding at least 10% of your base pay to the Roth TSP folder.

If you've heard of bull or bear markets, then you've probably realized the markets are cyclical. How do we know the market as a whole is priced high or low? The P/E ratio! Yes, you can use it for the whole market also. For historical long-term insights, I use a variation of the P/E called the Shiller P/E, developed by Robert Shiller at the University of Yale. All it does is take into account business expansion and contraction cycles.

As of 13 April 2016, the Shiller P/E was 26.1. This is 56.3% higher than the historical average of the Standard and Poor 500 index, which is 16.7.[17] Based on this ratio of how much a company's stock costs compared to how much money the company is making, the stock market on 13 April 2016 as a whole was overvalued. People were paying high prices to own US stocks. Another way to look at it is that when the market is priced high the chance it will go down is higher than the chance the market will go up based on historical averages.

People talk about not wanting to take risks, but if all they ever do is set their investments on autopilot and leave their money in the market even when it is grossly overvalued, then they are actually taking more risk. If you want to decrease your risk when the market is overvalued, take your money out of the stock market. Then when the market is undervalued, you can put the money back in. This is the basic principle of sell high and buy low. There are a few different techniques to make this happen.

Method 1: the advanced method—time the market. The technique I use is to time the market (gasp!). You can't time the market! It's impossible!

---

taken 9 April 2016

17   Shiller P/E—A Better Measurement of Market Valuation
www.gurufocus.com/shiller-PE.php
taken 6 April 2016

Despite what everyone says it is possible to time the market, within reason. No one can tell you what the market will do next week, or even next month. I believe you can make a reasonable guess for what the market will do over longer periods of time. In today's world, information is easily accessible. At a macro level, there is very little information a professional stock trader has access to that I don't also. Because I don't have to meet quarterly or even yearly quotas, I can afford to sit out of the market for years at a time. My money has been on the sidelines over a year now.

In May 2015, I sold at the top of the market. I was able to sell high. I assessed that the market was within a few months of the high one way or the other and felt the conditions were right to sell. The fact I sold my stocks at the actual high of the market was luck. Knowing the window made that possible. Millions of people do this by the way; I'm not the only one. For example, in July 2008, right before the great stock crash, TSP investors moved billions of dollars into the safer G fund after the market started going down.[18]

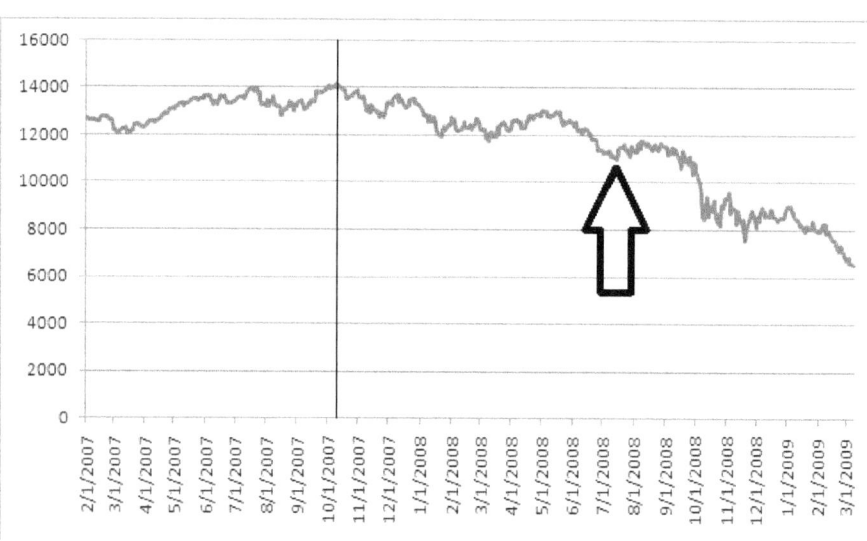

Chart 1. *Dow Jones Industrial Average (y-axis) over Date (x-axis)*

---

18 Following the Herd? TSP Investors Moving Billions into the G Fund www.fedsmith.com/2008/10/15/following-herd-tsp-investors-moving-billions taken 6 April 2016

Tens of thousands of investors put their money where their mouth was and moved their positions. Those not selling from the stock funds and buying into the treasury G fund saved over 40% of their retirement money in the following six months. Just doing this once makes a huge difference. If in July 2009, after the market had stabilized and started going back up, those same investors moved their funds back into the C fund, based off a $10,000 initial investment, in April 2016 they would have $22,300 versus $17,500.

Doesn't sound like a lot? What if we add another zero? $223,000 compared to $175,000. The difference is an F-150 within six years. Over 30 years the difference increases to $389,000 versus $305,000. One move would save almost $100,000 and I didn't use the top or bottom of the market. Selling in July of 2008 and buying in July of 2009 was easily achievable. The market was already moving in one direction and there were plenty of signs the trend was going to continue. You have to actually go and look at the signs.

The goal of this strategy is not to sell at the very top or buy at the very bottom. You can't possibly predict the market with that much specificity. However, you can sell within a few months or years of the top and buy within a few months or years of the bottom. For instance, in May of 2015 I transferred all of my TSP funds from the S and C funds into the G fund. The S and C funds are riskier and more volatile funds that track US company stocks. The G fund is government bonds and will only go up 2-3%. But the G fund has never decreased in value and is similar to cash. Despite what the professional financial world says, cash is a completely viable investment. Professional stock traders need investors like you and me to leave their money in the market, otherwise they don't get paid. They get a percentage of the money we investors give them to invest. So it is no wonder that dollar-cost averaging is the mainstream investment paradigm.

Yes, if I have most of my investments in cash I won't make as much money if the market goes up, but why risk it? Why pay more than a stock fund is worth? Why risk losing a large amount of money when the market goes down? People argue, "I have a long timeframe; I don't care if it goes down because I am in for the long haul." I am in the long game as well. Because I was able to time the market and move most of my funds into the safer G fund, like those other thousands of people, I was able to earn a higher percentage over time. If I can get just 3% more interest, as I showed earlier, over 35 years I will have more than doubled the amount of money. Doubling three or four million dollars is a LOT of money. Despite what the trillion-dollar investment industry has convinced you of (to their own financial benefit), you can time the market within reason, but you have to stay abreast of financial matters. I try to time the market to the right year, not the right week. If you are constantly trading then you will most likely revert to the average and pay a lot of money in fees.

Also, you can't just catch a news bite on TV or get one stock tip from a friend. You have to be invested in learning the truth. Knowing the truth is not for everybody. Some people are content to believe what they want to believe in their own little bubble world. That is fine if you want to live that way, but be honest with yourself and choose a different investment strategy.

If you don't enjoy reading about the stock market and listening to radio broadcasts and podcasts about the topic, then I recommend you use the simple rebalancing technique I explain next. If you do enjoy learning about the market, then there is huge money to be made in making your own investment decisions. It isn't rocket science and as long as your goals are long term and realistic it can be fruitful. From my own investing over the past five years, I have achieved an average annual return of 11.91% versus 8.49% from the highest returning TSP Lifecycle fund, the L2050. That doesn't sound like a lot but when I'm 65, that percentage difference will give me $3.5 million versus $1.6 million. Assuming I can maintain this advantage, I will have more than twice as much money when I retire. The L2050 fund will also decrease its returns as 2050 approaches while my investments will hopefully maintain their returns.

To earn millions of dollars, all you have to do is make learning about finance a priority. If you don't want to actually watch the market but still want to actively manage your money, then accept a little less return and use the following technique.

Method 2: the intermediate method—rebalance your TSP fund. The second technique to buying low and selling high is called rebalancing. It is very simple and no emotion is involved. People get emotional when it comes to money. We start getting greedy or fearful and the rational part of our brains shut off. My friend can't even talk about money or her heart starts racing and she gets anxious. I can tell when her pupils dilate. If this is you, then rebalancing is a fantastic way to manage your money. It is easy and there is no thinking involved.

All you do is maintain your portfolio at a certain asset percentage. A good starting point is 60% stocks (S and C funds) and 40% bonds (F and G fund). When the market does really well the stocks will increase in value so the percentage of stocks will increase. The stocks might grow to 70% of your portfolio and the bonds might shrink to 30%. Your TSP statement has a fancy little pie graph showing you the asset allocation. Twice a year, log into your TSP account and transfer the correct amount back.

In the example I gave, you would calculate 10% of your portfolio and move 10% from the S or C fund (either one you want; I have both equally weighted) into the G or F fund. Personally, I like the G since it doesn't have negative returns but the F fund is also an option. You move the right amount of stock funds into the bond funds to get it back to 60/40. When the stock market goes down the ratio will change the other way. You might be at 50% stocks to 50% bonds since the stocks move more than the bonds. They are more volatile. Then you sell the bonds and buy the stocks by simply transferring the money.

If you want to be more aggressive in order to get a higher return, then go to a 70/30 split or even 80/20. Or, if you think the market will go down, you can move your asset allocation to a more defensive ratio. For instance, I could limit my exposure to the market by going 30/70 stocks to bonds. If the market goes up instead of down, I still see some gains. If it does go down like I think it will, I only have 30% of my portfolio in stocks.

This is how rebalancing works, and it is an excellent way to buy low and sell high over a long period of time with no emotional involvement. You simply set it up and every six months, or once a quarter if you want, you go into your TSP and spend three minutes readjusting the ratios.

Method 3: the easy method—let someone else rebalance for you. If you don't want to even look at your money, then put all your money into a TSP Lifecycle fund. The Lifecycle fund manager continually rebalances the portfolio for you so you don't have to do anything. The longer the time before you need the money, the riskier the assets. This is the simplest technique since you literally don't have to do anything again with your TSP.

Even though you will most likely get a lower percentage rate (8.49%), you will still get a very good return on your money and it will automatically rebalance over the years. The biggest disadvantage to this technique, besides the lower rate of return, is you will not learn much about investing. You may not know a lot now, but just by reading this book you are showing you have an interest in it. Over many years, just like your net worth, your knowledge of how money works will increase exponentially. You do have to actually put some time into learning. The best way to do that is by actively investing and monitoring your assets. But, all in all, the Lifecycle funds are very well managed index funds. They will provide a great return on your money and not charge high fees like most other funds.

DEBT IS A TOOL: LEARN TO USE IT

Once you have the first two pools filling on automatic payments, retirement and college savings, you can start focusing on the third pool—wealth accumulation. The great advantage in filling the first two pools is you and your family are set for life. Once those pools are full, you could blow all your other money on lottery tickets and live in a van down by the river, still living a comfortable life in retirement. Your kids will still have access to a college education if they want it. If they don't want it, then you can immediately fund their entire retirement accounts for them.

If you really want a Ferrari at this point go ahead and get it. Your retirement is already funded and your kids will be taken care of. Now you can spend the money. The first two pools secure your financial future. You can blow the remaining money or you can use it to make more money.

Once the first two pools are full, my working-class friend says he will pay off all his debt. No debt is his idea of financial independence. That is fine for him, but the security of having my retirement and college savings accounts funded, allows me to be more aggressive with my non-retirement money. I can treat it like a game because the risks are lower. This doesn't mean I gamble with the money, but I am willing to make more aggressive investments to try to get as high a return as possible. If I pay the mortgage on my house, then I will get a guaranteed 3.25% interest return on my money (since that is the amount of interest I pay to the mortage lender). If my mortgage interest rate is 3.25%, and I pay sooner, I will be essentially getting an immediate 3.25% return on my money. The big negative is it's only a one time deal. After that, my money is just sitting in the house. Since my retirement and college savings are fully funded, I would rather use that money to get a possible 25% annual return than a guaranteed single return of 3.25%. I don't mind having debt as long as the debt provides a good possibility of making a lot more money.

Not all debt is bad debt. Guns may not kill people (people do), but they sure help. You can hunt with a bow but it is a lot more difficult. If your family depended on meat for survival, a rifle would be an invaluable tool. Despite what many people think, debt is not a bad thing. Debt is a very valuable tool you need to learn to use. There are different types of debt, but it all comes down to how much it costs you to borrow it and how you use it.

I keep mentioning interest rates again and again because they are so critical to increasing wealth. Based on interest rates at time of writing (April 2016), if the interest rate on your debt is over 4% it is bad debt no matter how you use it. You need to get rid of that debt or lower it through the techniques I explain in the credit section. If it is under 4% and you are using it for income-producing assets, then it is great debt. If it is under 4% and used on your car, then it can be either okay or bad debt depending on how expensive your car is. You need a car but do you need a $50,000 car?

Don't fear debt, fear bad debt. If debt is so bad, why does Apple, who currently has over $150 BILLION in cash, borrow money? They are borrowing money every time they sell a piece of stock. When a company goes public, they are selling a stake in their company for a price.

Imagine your cousin starts a lemonade stand and asks you to lend him money to buy the wood. You agree to give him the money but only if he agrees to give you a percentage of the profits the stand makes. You own a portion of the company. Stocks are the exact same thing. You are giving money to a company, and they are agreeing to give you a (small) percentage of the company. They are borrowing money from you for a promise of future returns (debt). Smart companies know how to use borrowed money to make more money. If they borrow a dollar to make two dollars, they just created an extra dollar they didn't have before.

The problem is people, and companies, using debt incorrectly. They borrow money to buy depreciating assets. That is just bad consuming and a poor person's mentality. Borrowing money to create more money is investing. That is a wealthy person's mentality. Just because knives can cut me doesn't mean I remove all knives from my life. It's pretty hard to eat a steak with a spoon.

I've heard people say proudly, "I have zero debt!" Great. I'm happy they set a financial goal and hit it, but I think they are hitting the wrong goal. If they have no debt but all their money is tied up in their house, then they will probably not end up nearly as wealthy as they could be. They think having less debt means their money is at less risk, but this is not necessarily true. Diversified income streams and a higher net worth create lower risk.

What if the housing market crashes again? All of their net worth is tied up in one single property. They may not owe any money on the house but they also can't access any of their money without moving or taking out a home equity loan which they will have to pay back with interest.

Yes, one of my rental houses could go vacant. They have in the past. Each house is only one income tributary. Even if one stream completely dries up, I still have other tributaries adding to the river. What happens if you need the money for some reason and all your money is tied up in your house? What if the opportunity of a lifetime presents itself to you? Even if your house goes way up in value you will have to move, take a home equity loan, or refinance to get the money out of it and that can take months. Honestly, I never want to fully own my house. It means a majority of my money is just tied up in bricks at my house. That money will get a historically low 3.25% return. No one got rich off a 3.25% return. You are literally putting the money into your mattress (home). I would rather have money out in the world making more money for me. A better goal to be proclaiming than being debt-free is "I hit $1 million net worth!" All rich people have debt. If they don't, then they aren't leveraging their money.

The best way to secure good, low interest debt is to have a high credit score. Your credit score sharpens (or dulls) your debt sword. People with high credit scores live in a bubble. The financial world treats them differently. The highest interest debt I have is my credit card at 9%. That's right 9%. That is higher than I have paid in the past eight years when it was 8.15%. My second highest interest debt is my mortgage at 3.25%, followed by my cars at 1.9%.

How did I get those numbers? Two ways. First I guard my credit like my bank account and second, I simply asked for a lower rate. If you get a quote and then start shopping that quote around, you will find the lowest rate. I actually could have gotten a lower car rate but I didn't want my car loan on a different web site.

In order to get good interest rates, you have to have good credit. A consumer with good credit is sought after by banks. Banks need to lend money in order to make money. Lending to people with good credit is like free money to them. When you have good credit they actively search you out. Everything is cheaper. Having amazing credit is like being a platinum medallion member for every airline. You don't wait in line and you get the best seats. It's one reason why the rich get richer.

To be wealthy you have to have good credit. Period. You can probably do it with bad credit but it will be much more difficult. In order to be a millionaire, unless you have a rich dad to give you millions of dollars like Donald Trump had, you are going to have to borrow money. If you have bad credit, borrowing money is going to be harder, if even possible, and it is going to cost a lot more. Like I showed earlier, a 1% difference in rate makes millions of dollars of difference in the end.

The financial industry almost doubled in size from 4.6% of the US economy in 1980 to 8.3% of the US economy in 2006.[19] That is a ginormous industry. Lending and investing money is almost 10% of the entire US economy. If you aren't paying attention to rates and fees, chances are you're paying hundreds of thousands of dollars to someone who is.

Getting and maintaining good credit is the easiest money you'll ever make. If your credit is below 600 I bet you can raise your score fifty points in a few weeks. There are only two steps to raising your score. First, you need to learn and keep track of your credit score. Second, you need to remove or dispute any negative factors.

Despite all the BS about being able to get free credit reports, I think it's just BS. It's not easy. If you don't know your credit score off the top of your head, chances are you tried to get one of those free reports and nothing happened. AnnualCreditReport.com will quickly and easily give

---

19 You're Making Your Financial Adviser Rich
www.bloombergview.com/articles/2016-04-11/those-tiny-fees-make-your-financial-adviser-rich
taken 12 April 2016

you all three of your credit reports for free, but you still have to pay $7.95 to learn you actual score. I pay $5 a month to my bank, USAA, for credit check and ID monitoring. It is a third-party service I access easily from my bank's website. I'm sure your bank offers it or you can get it direct from Experian. It tells me plainly what my credit score is and how I can improve it. When I first opened it I was surprised there were several negative factors listed. Some were incorrect. I fixed the correct ones by paying off debts I had forgotten about and then I disputed all the rest through the website. Having good credit is an amazing thing and I guard it like crazy. It literally took me 30 minutes to improve my score from good to great and I saved tens of thousands of dollars in lower interest.

For instance, I had a phone bill I thought I paid when I moved but the company did not receive my check. I found out four years later they had put a negative claim on my credit report. I paid the balance and called the company to ask nicely if they would remove the negative claim. I explained I was in the military and move very often. I had the money to pay it but just had made a mistake. The company removed the negative factor and my credit went up significantly.

After my score had improved I called USAA and asked if I could raise the credit limit on my credit card. I learned from the credit-check service having a higher credit limit was a positive factor in the credit score algorithm. The representative asked how high I wanted. I asked for the highest amount they would give me. The representative typed into his computer and said they could offer me $30,000. "Excuse me," I said, "it sounded like you said $30,000." My jaw dropped as he replied, "Yes, that is correct." Because my credit score was high in the first place the representative was able to raise my credit limit. Because he raised my credit limit my score went even higher. Raising your score initially will open up other opportunities to raise your score more.

Now this trick doesn't work if you max your credit card to $30,000. That would be financial suicide. So the idea is to have a high limit but only use what you can pay off each month because a low debt to limit ratio is a positive factor. Again, there are several services online that will give you your credit report and help you raise the score but you have to actually go and do it. Just remember how much money you will save and it can be fun.

I've talked to a few young airmen who don't have a credit card. Credit monitoring companies use your payment history to see how dependable a borrower you are. You need credit cards with no late payments to show you can handle credit and pay people back on time. As long as you use the saving system I explain in this book, you don't need to fear credit cards. You should definitely respect them. A lot of people have gotten into serious financial trouble through excessive credit card use. The magic of compounding interest works against you as well. If you can't pay the whole credit card bill off at the end of each month you are spending too much.

Another tip to avoid any negative factors on your credit is to have your bank autopay the minimum payment. This way even if you forget to pay a bill on time, you don't get hit with a late charge or, worse, a negative mark against your credit. Late payments are the number one negative factor on most people's credit history.

You need credit cards, but you don't need more than one you use on a regular basis. I have one Visa with cash back I use and one government card I have to have. I'm not a member of Air Force Clubs because they require you open a credit card to be a member. If you have to open a credit card to be a member of anything, then I recommend you skip it. There is a reason they offer you 100,000 airline miles to open a new credit card.

There are other ways to raise your credit score, but unfortunately some mistakes can only be fixed over time. After you fix everything you can fix on your report, you just have to keep making timely payments until the negative factors phase out. Your credit score will improve over time and soon enough you too will have excellent credit. The credit service tells you what you need to do and how to do it, so just follow the website. I am not a credit expert, but even after borrowing over $600,000 in mortgages my credit was 772. Before I got the last mortgage, it was over 815 for a few years. I was a gold medallion borrower. It took a while, but I just made an effort to improve it and track it over time.

Asking your bank representative, mortgage broker, or anyone else related to finance for discounts or a better deal pays off. I recently refinanced my rental properties. Initially I went with Wells Fargo since they held my mortgage and I wanted an interest rate reduction loan. I thought I had to go with them, but luckily I mentioned this to my mortgage broker.

He was able to get me a lower rate with lower closing costs. Just asking the question saved me thousands of dollars.

If you're in the military, USAA will lower your credit card rate to 4% for an entire year after you move. You fill out a form on their website and send in a copy of your move orders. It's almost free money. You do have to pay it back, so you still have to watch your spending, but it's a great deal. I don't know if other banks have this deal but everything is negotiable so ask. Whenever a representative asks, "Is there anything else I can do for you today?" say, "How can I lower my rates?" or "Are there any other campaigns or good deals I can take advantage of?"

START FILLING THE THIRD POOL WITH CASH FROM A BROKERAGE ACCOUNT

When you are ready to start building up money in a brokerage account, there are many tools on the internet to help you figure out what kind of portfolio you want to build. A good place to start is the Vanguard allocation tool personal.vanguard.com/us/funds/tools/recommendation. Fill out the forms with your time frame and risk tolerance, and it will come up with a decent fund allocation. Use one of the three investment methods I highlighted. Method 2, manual rebalance, is probably the best overall since you learn something about investing, but there is no emotion or possible mistakes involved. You simply maintain your asset allocation.

If the market crashes and you want to learn how to take advantage of it, I recommend the excellent book *One Up On Wall Street* by Peter Lynch. His basic argument is to invest in what you know and understand. If you are a huge Harley Davidson fan, you shouldn't just go and buy Harley stock (HOG). But you should investigate its fundamentals to see if it's a good investment.

If you had bought HOG back in July 2009 and sold last May when I sold, you would have seen a tenfold increase in your money. By the way, HOG has an impressive 3% dividend. It would be a great investment after the next crash since, initially, fewer people would be buying expensive motorcycles. But you know as a fan they will still make great bikes and the profits will return. You will be in a great position to analyze the industry.

Maybe you are an expert in handguns and ammunition, as many military members are. Smith and Wesson (SWHC) stock was beaten down starting in 2007 when they angered the whole gun community with their political views. Say you knew they still made great guns and sooner or later the gun buyers would forget about the company's evil ways and start

Start Filling the Third Pool with Cash from a Brokerage Account

buying again. The stock was flat because of this, even though the rest of the market was increasing rapidly. It didn't start increasing until Oct of 2012. If you bought SWHC then at $3 per share, you could have sold it in March of this year for $30 a share. In 3.5 years you could have turned $10,000 into $100,000.

I didn't know SWHC was going to increase and analysts on Wall Street didn't know either. Most of those people haven't even shot a gun. The point is you may be more of an expert in some things than you realize. As long as you keep your eyes open, opportunities like HOG and SWHC will show themselves. Opportunities like this are hard to find in an overpriced market, so wait until the market is undervalued based on the Shiller P/E.

You need liquid assets. Brokerage accounts give you access to liquid assets. Individual retirement accounts (IRAs) is are tax advantaged. They save you a huge amount of money in the long term, but there are penalties if you take the money out before you are 59 ½ years old. Once you have the first two pools filling up, in order to build wealth you can use now, the next thing you should do is call your bank and open a brokerage account. If you like a certain company's index funds you can also just open a brokerage account with them. I have referenced Vanguard several times because they have the cheapest rates and literally invented index funds. You can open a brokerage account with Vanguard online and set up automatic payments. If you are comfortable with index funds, since that is what the TSP uses, then your brokerage account with Vanguard will feel very similar.

How do you know a company is a good value? That's the million-dollar question—literally. If you can answer it, you will make millions of dollars. It doesn't take a genius to look at a balance sheet and determine if a company is doing well. Every public company has to give quarterly (Form 8-K) and annual reports (Form 10-K) including all their financial numbers. I first look at a company's broad fundamentals on the internet, usually at Yahoo finance. If you go to Yahoo finance and type in HOG, you will get access to all the information you need. The biggest initial indicator I look at is the P/E ratio. The P/E of HOG as of 18 April 2016 was a relatively low 12.72. If you compare this stock's P/E with its industry P/E, 19.1, HOG looks cheap. Since I feel like I understand the

HOG business model and the P/E is relatively cheap, I would call this stock a candidate for investment and start looking more deeply.

Once you have determined candidates for investing, look at their annual and quarterly filings. It's really not hard, and unless the company is lying, like Enron was, you can tell how the company is doing in less than five minutes. As an example, I skimmed through the 2015 Annual Report from Harley Davidson. I downloaded it from their website under SEC filings. You can also download these forms straight from the Yahoo finance page. Every public company is required to post these forms.

I learned immediately Harley sales in Europe and America decreased slightly in 2015, and they are losing market share in both these markets. Then I looked at the income table, which is in every quarterly or annual report I have looked at. I examined trends in earnings, which is otherwise known as net income. If you take the net income and divide by how many shares are out there you get the E in P/E. The market capitalization divided by net income also equals the P/E. I also research the assets, debt, and free cash the company has. Think of the company as a person. Income and assets are good. Debt and costs are bad. If debt and costs keep going up each year, and income and assets go down, the company is not doing well and you should probably not buy it. If you already own the stock, you should consider selling it. If, on the other hand, the stock is priced low and the opposite is true, income and assets are increasing while debt and costs are going down, then that is a buy (or hold) indicator.

Now let's look at HOG's income sheet fundamentals.[20]

A chart!! Run!!

Don't run. It's not complicated, just look at the chart.

---

20 HOG Form 10-K Quarterly SEC Filing
investor.harley-davidson.com/phoenix.zhtml?c=87981&p=irol-reportsannual
taken 13 April 2016

Start Filling the Third Pool with Cash from a Brokerage Account

(In thousands, except per share amounts)	2015	2014	2013	2012	2011
Statement of income data:					
Revenue:					
Motorcycles & Related Products	$5,308,744	$5,567,681	$5,258,290	$4,942,582	$4,662,264
Financial Services	$686,658	$660,827	$641,582	$637,924	$649,449
Total revenue	$5,995,402	$6,228,508	$5,899,872	$5,580,506	$5,311,713
Income from continuing operations	$752,207	$844,611	$733,993	$623,925	$548,078
Income from discontinued operations, net of tax	—	—	—	—	$51,036
Net income	$752,207	$844,611	$733,993	$623,925	$599,114
Weighted-average common shares:					
Basic	$202,681	$216,305	$222,475	$227,119	$232,889
Diluted	$203,686	$217,706	$224,071	$229,229	$234,918

(In thousands, except per share amounts)	2015	2014	2013	2012	2011
Earnings per common share from continuing operations:					
Basic	$3.71	$3.90	$3.30	$2.75	$2.35
Diluted	$3.69	$3.88	$3.28	$2.72	$2.33
Earnings per common share from discontinued operations:					
Basic	$—	$—	$—	$—	$0.22
Diluted	$—	$—	$—	$—	$0.22
Earnings per common share:					
Basic	$3.71	$3.90	$3.30	$2.75	$2.57
Diluted	$3.69	$3.88	$3.28	$2.72	$2.55
Dividends paid per common share	$1.240	$1.100	$0.840	$0.620	$0.475
Balance sheet data:					
Total assets	$9,991,167	$9,528,097	$9,405,040	$9,170,773	$9,674,164
Total debt	$6,890,388	$5,504,629	$5,259,170	$5,102,649	$5,722,619
Total equity	$1,839,654	$2,909,286	$3,009,486	$2,557,624	$2,420,256

(As you can see in the table HOG provides, total debt (second line from the bottom) increased dramatically in 2015 while total equity decreased). HOG did increase the dividend, which is a good sign of company health, but their earnings per share decreased in 2015. Each year before 2015, the earnings per share increased. A company's earnings is the most important thing. Companies exist to make money. If they don't make money, they are not fulfilling their purpose. When earnings stop increasing, or go negative, it is a very bad indicator.

In 2015, HOG's market share decreased, earnings per share decreased, and debt increased. The stock is cheap based on its P/E, which makes sense based on all the other negative fundamentals, but unless I thought HOG was going to do something amazing in the coming years, I would be looking for an opportunity to sell my position. This is how I make a basic determination of a stock's actual price. It takes no more than a couple minutes.

The key to picking stocks is remembering you are becoming a partial owner in the company. It doesn't just have to have a good product; it also has to be priced right. Wait until solid companies are on sale. This is most likely to happen when the Shiller P/E of the market as a whole is below its historical average, 16.7. The economy goes in cycles. Wait until a downturn to make your large investments and then, choosing the right stock becomes much easier.

Section 4
Real Estate

MAXIMIZE THE VA LOAN

Military personnel get an amazing benefit: the Veterans Affairs loan. Most people have to come up with 20% of the purchase price as a down payment on a house in order to buy it (without paying extra fees or mortgage insurance). On a $150,000 house that is $30,000 plus closing costs. In order to buy a $150,000 house, you would need around $35,000 in cash. Do you have $35k in cash? If you don't, you can still buy a house if you get access to the VA loan.

The VA will effectively front you the money. They don't give you the money; you still have to borrow the extra $30,000, but they will let you borrow the full value of the house, often at a lower rate than a normal civilian. This is a great benefit. I borrowed $400,000 on a 30 year fixed-rate mortgage at 3.00%.

You still have to buy a decent property at a good price, but it is harder than ever to overpay for a house. As a realtor, I have seen firsthand the VA appraisers will make sure you don't overpay for your house. Unless your realtor takes an active interest in helping you, no one will make sure you don't overpay the mortgage broker for the loan and the transaction. There are many predatory lenders out there. Every single lender calling you will be a veteran. They aren't all bad. I use a great lender who has consistently been honest and gotten me, my friends and my family the lowest lending rates at the lowest cost. This is what's important. His name is Casey Romijn and his information is found here: http://bit.ly/2cOAdeH. You should still check his rates against other lenders. I've found the 30 year FHA rates on mortgagenewsdaily.com to estimate the lowest VA loan rate available.

THE THREE ADVANTAGES OF REAL ESTATE OVER THE STOCK MARKET

Before we talk about how to use the VA loan to your best advantage, let's talk about why real estate is such a good long-term investment to begin with. There are three big advantages to real estate over the stock market.

Advantage 1: safe(er) leverage. Leverage is using borrowed money to generate investment returns. In the long term, real estate is an effective and relatively safe way to become wealthy. If you can buy a decent income-producing property with positive cash flow, it will make you a lot of money for relatively low risk. Yes, you can easily leverage stocks, but I believe it is more speculative than real estate. People will always need a place to live. The old adage is never buy a house you wouldn't want to live in. On the off chance the entire economy fails, if you own a house, at least you have a place to live. I have a few houses I wouldn't want to live in but I could if I had to.

Houses don't normally go out of business, but businesses go out of business all the time. As long as you buy in an area with a diversified income base, there is little risk of completely losing your asset. It is all about location, though, so the caveat is that the housing market where you are buying can't be dependent on one industry. My friend bought a house outside NASA's Houston base. It was the only major industry within miles. When NASA left, all the surrounding neighborhoods dried up. His house was basically worthless. He had to foreclose on it and it is still vacant years later. This is a major problem in small military towns. Buying in these towns is riskier than other areas but, because of this, they will have better buying opportunities. My friend bought a duplex outside of Eielson AFB in Alaska. Eielson was then suddenly on the BRAC list to be closed and the housing market there crashed. No one was buying.

Ultimately, Eielson didn't close and my friend has made a killing on his property. Since no one else would buy or build, there was no competition. Rental prices increased and he has made over $1,000 a month just in cash flow for ten years now.

Location is important, but so is big-picture timing. I have been investing in real estate and stocks for over sixteen years and I only have three properties. You can get wealthy owning real estate, but for the same investment I have found stocks provide a higher return on investment. To me, real estate is a way to safely leverage money and diversify my portfolio. I have cash, stocks, and real estate as my primary investments. Stocks provide the growth and true wealth production, while real estate provides a consistent long-term return on money and tax benefits.

Advantage 2: the government wants you to own a house. In order to help make this possible, they subsidize 30-year fixed rate mortgages. Few other places in the world offer 30-year loans. During my previous assignment in Turkey, every pilot I met owned a house. The amazing difference there is they have to put 25% down for the house, and then they have five years to pay the rest back at 20% interest! Can you believe that? They were blown away when I tried to explain the 30-year mortgage. Not one of them believed me. Their government does not support housing ownership like ours does. If they weren't subsidized by the federal government, our mortgages would be like car loans, short term.

It doesn't stop there; the government also provides tax advantages for owning a home. All the interest you pay on your mortgage is tax-free. Meaning money you pay to borrow the money comes right off your income. This is why having all your money in your house is a bad use of money. Not only can you borrow the money at a ridiculously low rate and put almost nothing down to borrow it, all the interest you pay on the loan is tax-free. If you can get a measly 2% return on your money you are ahead. The one caveat is if you are disciplined and can get a good rate, a home equity line of credit (HELOC) can get money out of your house. Cory Carmichael, the retired enlisted airmen who reached well over $1 million net worth, used a HELOC effectively. It's like a lower interest loan you can use to buy other things, but it can get you into trouble. Talk to a lender about your options if you are in this situation.

Advantage 3: capital appreciation. Similar to stocks, houses will hopefully increase in value over time, although houses can't go up in price forever because people will always need an affordable place to live. If you can get positive cash flow on your property, then the tenant is paying your mortgage while the house increases in value over time.

Whenever house prices in an area go up, rental prices also go up. So your rental income increases along with the equity in your house (since the value went up). The added benefit of this is you don't have to put too much money down to get this benefit.

Let's say you buy a property for $300,000. Does this sound like a lot? You need to start thinking bigger. You have a VA limit of $417,000. As long as you qualify (you need good credit), then you can borrow the full amount. For almost nothing down you can own this property. Let's say you rent the house and are able to just break even after all your costs. You have neutral cash flow. If the house value increases just 3% in a year, which is completely normal, you will have increased your net worth by $9,000.

Remember, on each mortgage payment, you are paying some of the principal down. This means on a $300,000 loan at 3.25%, after the first year you would have paid $4,500 of the principal of the loan back. So in one year, the house would have increased your net worth by $13,500 on a $0 investment ($9,000 + $4,500). And each year it gets better. If you can get a 3% property appreciation the second year, then the equity increases $11,700 (3% of $309,000) and the principal increases to $6,150 for a total of $17,850. Assuming rental income remains the same and you are still breaking even with the rent and costs, the second year you increase your net worth $17,850. In two years you will have increased your net worth by $31,350 and put no money down. That is the power of real estate.

The US government provides an amazing benefit with the VA loan. If you are lucky enough to be eligible, then follow the basic guidelines in this section to maximize your benefit. The VA loan gives you a great financing option for zero money down, but it won't find the right property for you. Knowing the three rules of real estate will make sure you buy the right property at the right time.

THE THREE RULES OF REAL ESTATE

Before you can find the right property to maximize your VA loan benefit (which we'll discuss in the next chapter), you have to understand the three rules of real estate.

Rule #1 of buying real estate: DON'T OVERPAY FOR A PROPERTY. Period. This is by far the most important rule for buying real estate. You only have one chance to buy a property. Make it count. The price you paid for a property will always be the same. Decades later you will still have paid that price. I don't care how much you love the property. Don't overpay. There are millions of properties out there. Find one with positive cash flow or wait for the market to improve.

Overall market timing makes a difference. I never invest in an asset class when I hear about it from three unrelated sources within a day. When everyone around you is buying something and making money, there is huge peer pressure to get in on the action. The problem is, when more people start buying, they drive the prices higher. Sooner, rather than later, the asset is overpriced. If you hear about an asset class (stocks or housing) from three unrelated sources within a short period of time, get out of that market.

For instance, back in 2006, everyone and their brother were buying houses. You couldn't get away from it. Everywhere I went, people were talking about how much money they or someone they knew had made off a house. Or they were explaining how they had just purchased the perfect property and there was no way they could lose. Then in 2007, the market crashed.

In the run up to the Dotcom bubble of 1999, everyone was talking about investing in stocks. So much easy money was being made! If you don't get in the market you are going to miss out! Guess what? You already missed out.

If normal everyday people are talking about an investment class, it is already oversold. Most normal people don't talk about investing for investing sake. People like you and me who are interested in becoming wealthy, talk about investing. Normal people talk about sports and buying stuff, not investing and saving. If this changes and the common conversation around the water cooler is about real estate or stock investing, get out while you can. Don't just walk, run.

The perfect time to buy is when things can't possibly get any worse. It's like the wars in Syria, Iraq, and Afghanistan right now. We are still fighting there but even the news outlets are tired of reporting on it. It's just dragging on and on. That is when you need to strike, when hope is gone and people don't even want to hear about it.

No one wanted to invest in the stock market in 2009. Everyone I knew was depressed that their investment accounts were so low they didn't even want to talk about it. This is the perfect time to invest. Not right when it's going down, but after it's down and has stayed down. The horse died and has been beaten for a while.

After the housing crash of 2007–2008 no one wanted to buy a house. What, are you crazy? Have you seen how much money people just lost? But that was a great time to buy because there were great deals to be found.

You don't have to time every market low point. You just need to time one. So the first rule of buying investments, and especially in the case of houses and stocks, is don't buy when everyone is hyped about the market. Don't even think about. That is actually the perfect time to sell.

I am explaining this in this section because real estate is harder to off-load. If the stock market starts tanking and I realize I made a mistake, in less than a minute I can sell my entire position. But with real estate it takes months to off-load a property, and only if someone wants to buy it. There is (almost) always a stock buyer somewhere in the world. I can sell stocks from my cell phone in a few minutes.

As long as you buy a piece of property at a good price, it is a safe investment. If you close on a property at a price it is not actually worth or you buy when the market in general is overpriced, you are at higher risk.

Rule #2 of buying real estate: shop the loan first. Everyone shops the house. For hours and hours, they scour the internet looking for houses. They want a certain type of kitchen countertop. They want a three-car garage. They want their guests to have a private bathroom. The list goes on. But when it comes to financing they spend two minutes securing the loan. This blows me away.

As a hobby, in order to learn more about the game, I am a real estate agent in my free time. Yes, I have to skip watching TV and work at night or on the weekends, but I learn about real estate and get paid for my time. I have seen people argue, to the point of losing a deal, over a few hundred dollars. They simply don't think they should pay for the Home Owners' Association transfer. That is just too far.

When it came to the rate on their loan, one simple number that could have saved them hundreds of dollars each and every month, they took the first quote. Before you even start looking at properties, you should get no fewer than ten mortgage quotes. Seriously, more than ten. If you haven't learned by now, percentage points matter. Slap yourself and yell, "PERCENTAGE POINTS MATTER!! AAHHH!!" Because they matter. With a longer time frame, they matter even more. So let's talk about how to know a mortgage is cheap.

The cost of a loan is all about the annual percentage rate (APR). After all the predatory lending practices of the housing crises, the federal government did a great job reforming the industry. Now, as long as you take at least a passive interest in the cost of the loan, you can easily shop loan prices. You still have to look. The government can only protect you so much; you have to try a little.

Before giving you a loan, the government requires lenders to issue you an estimate. This estimate use to be called a Good Faith Estimate (GFE) but was changed in 2015 to the Loan Estimate (LE). The most important number on there is the APR. This is the actual percentage rate you will pay after all loan costs are factored in. The APR includes the interest rate from the lender and all the other fees and points to get the loan.

One trick mortgage brokers do is they will say, "I can get you 3.25%." Great, except that might not be the APR. The actual rate may be 4.0%

but if you pay extra money at the beginning you can buy interest points down to 3.25%. All this means is you are paying the lender cash money at the beginning in order to lower your rate a little each month. It's like putting more money down on a car to get a lower payment each month. You are still paying more for the car in the end but your monthly payments are lower.

Lenders have to disclose how much they are charging but they don't have to advertise it or tell you outright on the phone. This fee, the loan origination fee, can be anywhere from $295 to $9,000. I promise mortgage brokers don't do their job for your benefit. Like all salesmen, they are paid to make a profit for the company. I have found a great mortgage broker I trust, but I asked for twelve quotes in order to find him.

The two questions you should ask any prospective lender are: What is the APR? And how much is it going to cost me? Ask enough mortgage brokers those two questions and you will find the cheapest loan. I heard several mortgage brokers say money is money, so it doesn't really matter where you get it, the costs will be the same. Don't believe them. Those mortgage brokers gave me .75% higher quotes.

Remember you are the customer, and they need to get mortgages or they don't get paid. You have all the leverage. Don't let them keep you on the phone with a bunch of random questions. Either they have the lowest rate or they don't.

A broker can determine the current rate in about ten seconds with just your income and your credit score. If your credit is bad then you need to first fix your credit, but once your credit is decent (over 650) you hold all the cards. Brokers need to earn your business. If they start asking for more information, tell them you have to go and thank them for their time. They can send you an email or text with the quote when they get it. Once I get a lower quote I go back through the top contenders and see if they can beat it. Do you know a quicker and easier way to make thousands of dollars?

Rule #3 of real estate: buy a property with positive cash flow from the beginning. Cash flow is the rent minus all the costs. Cash flow is what you have left over after you take the rent and pay the property manager, the bank, the taxes, and any maintenance fees. If money is leaving your hands, then you have negative cash flow. If money is coming in, you have positive cash flow.

The easiest way to make sure you have positive cash flow is to buy a fourplex. If I could go back, the only thing I would do differently is, during my first assignment, I would have used the VA loan to buy a fourplex and live in one of the units. This technique is so powerful for a few reasons.

First, as long as you plan to live in one of the units, you can use your VA loan. (If you don't plan to live in the property you will not be able to use a VA loan and you will also get an investor loan rate which is usually about a percentage point higher.) If you buy the fourplex with a VA loan, you've bought four rental properties without putting any money down. Four units is the maximum number of units you can finance with a residential or VA loan. If you want to buy a property that has over four units, you have to use a commercial loan and VA is not allowed. Commercial loans require more cash down and give you less protection from loss. I've never used commercial financing.

A VA loan requires you live in the property for some amount of time but in the military our plans change all the time. How many times have you been scheduled to move but delayed? How many times have you been moved ahead of schedule? Don't fret too much about the time frame. Just ask your lender what their requirements are. You should be shopping the loan before you put an offer down on a property anyway.

If you think you are going to move soon but don't have orders yet, technically you haven't been ordered to move, so I think you should still be able to use this government-provided benefit. If you buy a house and then get orders to move the next day, what are you supposed to do? You have to move in the military and the VA understands this. Just focus on using your benefit. If the VA doesn't allow you to buy the house, as long as you asked this before you put an offer down there will be no problems.

Finally, the largest benefit of a fourplex over a single family home is cash flow. When it comes to rental property, cash flow is king. More units make more cash flow. My buddy is able to get $1,000 of income out of his duplex because it is a duplex. If it was a single family home, he would only get $500 a month. He gets double the income for the same initial investment.

Imagine you bought a fourplex and are just breaking even. Over the course of a year the rents go up $25 a month in your area. This is a marginal amount but all of a sudden you have $75 of free cash flow every month. That is almost $1,000 a year and the rent in your area only went up a measly $25. After you move, you will have four units to rent out. If the rent goes up another $25 over the next few years all of sudden you are making $150 every month. That is $2,400 a year of income and you didn't have to do anything but accept the risk of ownership.

At my first base, I bought a rental house with a buddy. Over the following fourteen years the rent went up $250. That is good, I see an additional $125 a month. But imagine if I had bought a fourplex on my own. Let's say rent went up only $200. Now I would have an additional $800 a month in income. That is almost $10,000 a year! All I did was buy a different type of property. We are talking hundreds of thousands of dollars over time.

Before we go further, I don't recommend you go in with anyone else. If you can't afford to own a property on your own because the monthly costs are too high, then you are buying the wrong property. For instance, that first house cost us $200 a month to rent out because the rent did not cover all the costs of ownership. We did not shop the loan and accepted the first mortgage loan quote. We did not check rental prices in the area. It was an incorrect purchase.

Only buy a property you know you can at least break even on right from the beginning. Fourplexes provide less risk to own because they bring in more rent each month, and the chances of every unit going vacant at the same time is extremely low. If a house goes vacant for two months a year, you lose a lot of money and it is very stressful. But, if one unit in a fourplex goes vacant two months a year, you are still making money and it is not nearly as stressful.

If you still can't help yourself and decide to go with a partner (I did, after all), then never go in with more than one person. The math just doesn't make sense. If you go 50/50 with someone you reduce the risk 50%, but you have to deal with another person's desires and drawbacks, and you only make 50% of the profit. If you add a third person you each split 33% of the investment risk but you have to deal with a third person. For only 17% savings (50%-33%) you are putting yourself at much more risk.

You will have to deal with this extra person for potentially decades while you own the house. What if they have a terrible divorce and their ex-wife comes after their assets? That asset is also your asset. What if they don't want to kick in money for a new roof? What if you want to sell but they don't? You have to have a unanimous decision to do anything.

Yes, you might be great friends now, but people change over time. Relationships change. Why put extra pressure on your friendship anyway? Finally, if those reasons aren't enough, you only get 33% of the profit. 100% is way better, even if it is on a smaller property.

How much is an investment property actually worth? An investment property's value completely depends on how much cash flow it can produce. You can get cash flow from a property by either renting it out or by selling it. I don't buy and sell houses to make short-term profit because of one major limitation of real estate: the transaction costs are very high.

When I bought my first house I was amazed at how many people were making money off the deal. People I had never met, doing jobs I had never heard of, took my money. No wonder we have housing bubbles—so many different people make money when you buy and sell a house. The bank, the mortgage broker, two real estate agents, the inspector, the termite inspector, the appraiser, the VA, the title agent, the title insurance company, Uncle Sam, and a partridge in a pear tree all get paid when a house is bought or sold. It's ridiculous. Eleven different entities make money off your investment and they don't even have an ownership interest. Most of them could care less what the price of the property is. The ones that do care make more money if the price is higher.

To make money on a rental, the rent must at least cover all of the costs to own the property. This includes the cost of a property manager, if you don't want to manage the property yourself. I have had rentals for fifteen years and never had to personally deal with a client. To me, it is just not worth the headache. Property managers normally charge 8–10% of the monthly rent and believe me it is worth it. If you can get around this fee then by all means do it, but if you don't live in the local area or don't want to deal with tenants then just buy a property that will still make money after you pay the property manager. Remember to shop the property managers and negotiate a lower rate. They are not all created equal.

FINDING THE RIGHT PROPERTY

Don't start shopping until you know how much money you have to work with. Don't waste your time looking at properties if you haven't shopped the loan yet. Unlike in the past, when lenders gave millions of dollars to people who couldn't handle it, today the lenders have to adhere to strict debt-to-income levels. If you haven't fixed your credit yet, you may not be able to get the money and shopping around for properties will just be a practice exercise. According to a very experienced high net worth (HNW) banker, even HNW clients can't get loans without cash and good credit. So the bottom line is this: before you talk to a realtor and start looking at properties, get a pre-approval from the lender.

The two main requirements for a good rental property are positive cash flow and minimal problems from tenants. For an in-depth explanation of real estate investing, I recommend the excellent book, *The Millionaire Real Estate Investor*.[21]

The first requirement is you must have a positive, or at least neutral, cash flow from day one. You cannot control the future value of your property but you can control what you pay for it when you buy it. Thus, cash flow needs to be positive right from the beginning. If you estimate cash flow will be negative, then choose a different property or offer a price that will give you positive cash flow. If you can't get positive cash flow, it is most likely not a great investment and you can make better use of your money and time somewhere else.

The second property requirement I look for is a reasonable level of "headacheness." Yes, I just made that word up, but the point is you don't want to deal with an old dirty property attracting tenants who will not treat

---

21   The Millionaire Real Estate Investor
www.amazon.com/The-Millionaire-Real-Estate-Investor/dp/0071446370
taken 22 April 2016

it well. Or, if you are dealing with a lot of issues, you better be making a ton of money. Even if you have a property manager, when a tenant breaks something or skips the rent, you will have to deal with the lost payments or maintenance costs. The better the neighborhood, the better the tenants. Good neighborhoods attract honest, considerate, rent-paying people but those neighborhoods are also more expensive to buy in.

In general, lower-income housing is riskier but much more lucrative. The key to finding the right property is to balance the two requirements based on your needs. You want a property that is making money but has an acceptable amount of headache. In general, the nicer the property and the neighborhood, the less headache for you and your property manager but the less money you will make.

You can change anything about a property except its location, so you want to get this right. You can knock an entire house down and build a big brand-new house in its place, but it's still in the same place. This is why the old adage of "location, location, location" exists.

You want to buy in an up-and-coming neighborhood, a neighborhood that used to be bad but is now transitioning to a cool and hip place to live. It's basically a neighborhood with bars on the windows of old businesses and houses but they aren't needed anymore. The new businesses and houses don't have bars on the windows because it is an unnecessary expense. The pawn shops are closing and in their place coffee shops and other service oriented small businesses are opening.

These types of neighborhoods are usually more centrally located in cities. I'm sure you have seen houses converted to businesses. Any place you see a small law firm in an old cute house was most likely a transitional neighborhood. It's already transitioned by that point and it is probably too late to invest in the neighborhood, but it gives you a clue as to what to look for in other areas.

Once you've decided on an area to start looking, use the internet to figure out the rental rates and compare those to the purchase price of any for-sale properties. If you estimate the property can make close to .7% of the purchase price per month in rent, then put it on the candidate list. For instance, if you are looking at houses priced at $100,000, then the rent in that area needs to be close to $700 per month or it's not even worth looking into the house. The higher you can get this ratio the better. You will find very quickly the more rental units in a property, the easier it is to make positive cash flow.

As an example, I recently helped a friend buy a rental property. They bought a cute little 3-bed, 2.5-bath townhome in a sought-after neighborhood. They were able to purchase the house for $178,000 and rented it out within a couple months for $1200 per month. This comes out to .67% (1200 divided by 178,000). It's not quite .7% but it was enough for them to have neutral cash flow right from the beginning.

This ratio will depend on several variables: the mortgage interest rate, local property taxes and HOA fees, rental insurance, and property manager fees. Including all of those fees, at $1200 a month in rent, they still have a $40 positive cash flow per month to cover yearly maintenance or minimize the pain of any vacancies. If they do get any vacancies (you should plan for two months vacant per year), they will be in the red slightly for their investment. But remember, each month they are able to claim the mortgage interest off their taxes, and they are paying about $300 to the principal of the loan.

It can be difficult to figure out if you are making money on a rental property, so just focus on the cash flow. A neutral cash flow means you are approximately breaking even. A positive cash flow means you are making money.

Now let's assume my friend spent $100K more and purchased a fourplex for $278,000. I found a fourplex for that price so let's look at the difference. The fourplex is actually two duplexes on the same lot of land. There are two 3-bed, 1-bath units and two 2-bed, 1-bath units. He could live in one of the 3-bed units. Based on the owner-entered information, he would get $1950 per month in rent from the other three units. Since he has never managed property before, he would hire a property manager to take care of any tenant issues. Assuming he gets a VA loan on the full $278,000 at 3.5% interest, he would have $250 positive cash flow each month after he pays all the monthly costs I mentioned above. Not only would he pay no rent to live there, he would also get paid $250 each month to live there.

Meanwhile, each month he is paying $438 straight to the principal on the loan and he can deduct the $811 of mortgage interest he pays each month off his taxes. I would recommend he save the $250 and the money he would have paid in rent in a slush fund for the property. A slush fund is a few thousand dollars set aside so when there are maintenance requirements or vacancies, and there will be both, he doesn't have to worry since he already has $4000 set aside. In six months he will able to save $1500 from the cash flow alone, not to mention any money he would have paid in rent.

Here is the best part: when he moves, he has an income-producing property. Ta-da! Now he has a property making $250 a month plus the rent from his unit, approximately $850. His cash flow is now $1100 per month. That is over $13,000 per year of straight income not to mention the tax benefits or the real estate appreciation. If the property goes up just 3% in a year, which is forecast for the Phoenix area, he makes another $8,500 per year in equity. In one decent year of ownership he can add over $20,000 to his net worth in cash and equity. And once the property is set up with a good property manager there is little to nothing he needs to do. This is the power of the VA loan. He was able to do all of this with literally no money down.

The only real negative to VA loans is you have to pay a straight VA funding fee which can be several thousand dollars. For the first house, it is 2.15% of the purchase price for regular military and 2.4% of the purchase price for reserves and National Guard.[22] For our $278,000 house, that is $6,000 for regular military and $6,700 for reserve and National Guard members in fees to the VA. This money is rolled into the loan, but you still have to pay it back.

The more money you put down on the house, the less you pay in terms of the funding fee. On the first house, if you put 5% down, the funding fee decreases from 2.15% to 1.5%. So on our $278,000 house if you put $13,900 down you save $1,800 in VA funding fees. That is a 13% percent return on your money, so if you can't find anything better to do with the

---

22   Funding fee tables
www.benefits.va.gov/homeloans/documents/docs/funding_fee_table.pdf
taken 26 April 2016

cash (such as during an overvalued stock market), then putting down 5% is a good idea.

On any subsequent VA loans, the fees go up. If you don't put any money down on a subsequent purchase, even if you sold the first one to gain your full eligibility back, the VA charges a 3.3% funding fee. On our $278,000 that is $9,174 straight onto the price of the house. If you put down 5% of the purchase price the fees go from 3.3% down to 1.5% (1.75% for reserves). Now your $13,900 down payment will save you $5,000. That is an immediate 36% return on your money. This is money well spent so after the first VA loan, you should do your best to get the money for a 5% down payment.

You actually don't need to sell your first home to take advantage of the VA loan benefit. You have a couple different options to maximize your VA loan benefit. Know your VA eligibility limits. Each military member has a $417,000 limit to their VA eligibility, but you can go above this amount if you put down 25% of the difference. As an example, my friend could buy the property we discussed with no money down and use $278,000 of his $417,000 limit. When he moves, he can buy another property for $139,000 with no money down and reach his limit of VA eligibility (278K+139K=417K).

He will pay the full 3.3% funding fee on his second purchase, but he will not have to put any cash down. But let's say, instead of the $139,000 house, he wants a more expensive house. Let's say he found the exact same fourplex in a different area for the same price as his first house, $278,000. He can still purchase this property using the rest of his VA eligibility, $139,000, but he will have to put down 25% of the excess amount. In this case, the excess amount is $139,000 ($278K+$278K-$417K=$139K), so he would have to put down 25% of that, or $34,750.

Remember he is putting more money down, so the funding fee decreases. Since he is putting over 10% down on this property, the funding fee goes to 1.25%. On his $34,750 he saves $5,700. This is still a 16% immediate return on his money. If we can get over 15% return on our money, we will be rich, so he should definitely find the cash from somewhere to put the money down on the second house.

Although $34,750 is a lot of cash to have lying around, this money goes straight to the principal and is still $25,000 less than what he would have to put down without the VA loan (20% of the full $278,000 home). But he is already getting $13,000 in cash from the first house, and he didn't have to put any money down to get it. If he saves his money, instead of buying fancy cars or other depreciating assets, he can purchase a second fourplex for $15,000 less than the cost of a new truck.

He may not be able to do this on his next assignment. Maybe he waits a few years to build the budget, but a few deployments or bonuses should make this cash available at some point in his career. You don't need more than two or three fourplexes before you start making serious money. An extra $26,000 a year from two fourplexes on top of your pension of $40,000 is enough to retire at 40 years old if you want. This doesn't include TSP or retirement savings. If you pick a decent fourplex with positive cash flow and purchase it with sound financing, you can set yourself up for life. Two fourplexes provide almost as much income as 20 years in the military. It only takes $35,000, some basic knowledge about loans and real estate, and some calculated risk.

SUMMARY - TAKE IT ONE STEP AT A TIME

Step 1 - Set up the TSP for military, or 401(k) for civilian, to save 10% of your base income. Don't overthink this step. Just do it and start filling up the first pool: retirement.

Step 2 - Create an Excel spreadsheet and start tracking your net worth. Input your email at my website at chrislehto.com and I will send you an excel spreadsheet you can use to get started. It's free.

Step 3 - Set up credit-check monitoring and improve your credit.

Step 4 - If you have, or are planning to have children, open a 529 account and start automatic payments. I recommend $300 a month per child in the Vanguard 529 plan in Nevada but any amount helps. There are other 529 plans out there with low fees and decent returns so do a little research if you don't want to just pick my recommendation. This is the second pool: college savings.

Step 5 - Look at the real estate market in your area or your next move location, and figure out if purchasing a duplex or fourplex will provide positive cash flow. If there are properties available where you can make immediate positive cash flow, then use your VA loan to purchase and live in the property. If you can't make neutral cash flow, then don't buy. Rent a house and wait until the market improves or you move to a better location.

Step 6 - Start automatically saving whatever cash you have left over in a brokerage account. This step and Step 5, real estate and stocks in a brokerage account, are the third pool: current wealth accumulation.

Step 7 - Continue to learn and have fun winning the game. For instance, I do my own taxes using TurboTax. It really isn't difficult, and I learn where I pay the most taxes. If you always pay someone else to do your financial business for you, you won't learn the underlying processes. To me, learning is fun, especially when it will make me hundreds of thousands of dollars in the future.

You are off to a great start by simply reading this book. Not just because it has amazing things in it benefiting you and your family (though I hope it does), but because reading this book means you are taking an active role in learning about money. I love reading anything about money: interest rates, mortgage rates, tax benefits, insurance benefits, stock analyzing, etc. I love learning new things, and unlike pretty much anything you learned in school, knowing these things will make you, your family, and your friends more money.

For instance, two years ago I had a conversation with an Embassy worker who approved visas for Israelis in Jerusalem. He complained many Israelis, who had never stepped foot onto American soil, were able to claim George W. Bush's child tax benefit (which is $1000 for each dependent child). I was immediately outraged these foreigners were taking our tax money. He had repeatedly brought it up to Congress, but they couldn't change the law. It is a loophole designed to let Americans adopt children from overseas. The positives outweigh the negatives, so Congress was unable to change the law.

A year later, I explained this phenomenon to an American friend of mine living overseas. He followed my advice to do his taxes in America and apply for the credit. He received a check for $12,000 (three kids over a four-year period). He placed the $12,000 in his children's college savings plan. One tip will pay for one year of college for each of his three children. Knowing how money and benefits works allows you to provide for yourself, your family, and your friend's families.

As another example, while I was reading about IRAs, I found a federal benefit called the Savers Credit. This allows you to get a government match of up to 50% of your IRA contributions if your adjusted gross income is less than $30,000.[23] After ten years, I finally convinced my

---

23   Retirement savings contributions credit (saver's credit)
www.irs.gov/Retirement-Plans/Plan-Participant,-Employee/
Retirement-Savings-Contributions-Savers-Credit
taken 3 May 2016

sister to start saving for retirement. She made a free $1000 using the Savers Credit, all because she knew the correct information. Information is power. When it comes to money, knowing how money works will make all the difference.

In order to learn about money, you will have to find a way to continue learning about it that you enjoy. Reading and talking about it is okay, but the only way to truly master it is to do it. You can't learn to swim by never getting wet. If you're too scared to make deals and take calculated risks, then you will never get in the game and actually learn how money works. You need to be smart about it and not just jump into the deep end right away, but you do need to get in the game. Do what you need to do to prepare, but get out there and make some mistakes. Chances are, you are already making huge financial mistakes by simply not monitoring your credit and not saving enough for retirement. If you fix these two things, you are 90% of the way to being well off.

If you follow the basic guidelines in this book, you can make a few mistakes because the big-picture finances will be taken care of. If you have a fully funded retirement because you started right when you entered the military or the work force, you have more flexibility to take risks later on. If you started late or are now just starting to fund your retirement, that's okay. The best thing you can do is start. Even if I lose all my rental houses and everything I own right now, I still have my retirement funded and my kids' education paid for.

BECOME A MILLIONAIRE- START TODAY

If you feel a little overwhelmed after reading this book, that is okay. The more deals you do and the more books and articles you read, the more comfortable you will become with all the financial terms and vehicles.

In 2014, ten million American households had a net worth over one million dollars.[24] Why not be one of them? Cory Carmichael retired from the enlisted core and grew his net worth to well over a 1.5 million dollars. Why not you also?

I've created a free downloadable action plan you can follow immediately to reach a $1 million net worth. It won't happen overnight, it will take years, but if you simply print and follow the action plan, you are guaranteed to become a millionaire.

Don't overthink it! You can be rich, just print the action plan and follow it. Good luck!

Go here to get the free action plan: chrislehto.com/actionplan

---

24   More Millionaires than ever are living in the US
www.cnbc.com/2015/03/09/more-millionaires-than-ever-are-living-in-the-us.html taken 25 June 2016

REFERENCES

(1) How Many Homeowners Have Paid Off Their Mortgages?
fivethirtyeight.com/datalab/
how-many-homeowners-have-paid-off-their-mortgages
taken 23 March 2016

(2) Rage Against the Machine
en.wikipedia.org/wiki/Rage_Against_the_Machine
taken 23 March 2016

(3) Stock Return Calculator with Dividend Reinvestment for Every Stock
dqydj.net/stock-return-calculator-dividend-reinvestment-drip
taken 23 March 2016

(4) Edmunds.com
www.edmunds.com/ford/f-150/2014/for-sale/
az/buckeye/?radius=50&trim=King%20
Ranch&mileage=24000:38000&invtype=USED&src=clus-
ters_1458754453406_9x2
taken 23 March 2016

(5) How much would taxes be on $1 million?
www.ask.com/business-finance/
much-would-taxes-1-million-b781ab5e2fdff6c4
taken 23 March 2016

References

(6) Ten important Facts about Capital Gains and Losses
www.irs.gov/uac/
Ten-Important-Facts-About-Capital-Gains-and-Losses
taken 23 March 2016

(7) Why Mitt Romney and Other Wealthy Investors Pay Less Taxes
www.salary.com/
why-mitt-romney-other-wealthy-investors-pay-less-taxes
taken 23 March 2016

(8) Military pension calculator
militarypay.defense.gov/Calculators/ActiveDutyRetirement/
High36Calculator.aspx
taken 23 March 2016

(9) Do We Need $75,000 a Year to Be Happy?
content.time.com/time/magazine/article/0,9171,2019628,00.html
taken 23 March 2016

(10) State and Local Sales Tax Rates in 2015
taxfoundation.org/article/state-and-local-sales-tax-rates-2015
Taken 25 June 2016

(11) Wheat and chessboard problem
en.wikipedia.org/wiki/Wheat_and_chessboard_problem
taken 30 March 2016

(12) Chasing Warren Buffett's Alpha
blogs.cfainstitute.org/investor/2012/09/11/
chasing-warren-buffett-alpha
taken 2 April 2016

(13) Harvard at a Glance

www.harvard.edu/about-harvard/harvard-glance

taken 2 April 2016

(14) What's the Price Tag for a College Education?

www.collegedata.com/cs/content/content_payarticle_tmpl.jhtml?articleId=10064

taken 8 April 2016

(15) How the $1.2 Trillion College Debt Crisis is Crippling Students, Parents and the Economy

www.forbes.com/sites/specialfeatures/2013/08/07/how-the-college-debt-is-crippling-students-parents-and-the-economy/#481a637d1a41

taken 9 April 2016

(16) What is your tax bracket?

www.bankrate.com/calculators/tax-planning/quick-tax-rate-calculator.aspx

taken 9 April 2016

(17) Shiller P/E—A Better Measurement of Market Valuation

www.gurufocus.com/shiller-PE.php

taken 6 April 2016

(18) Following the Herd? TSP Investors Moving Billions into the G Fund

www.fedsmith.com/2008/10/15/following-herd-tsp-investors-moving-billions

taken 6 April 2016

References

(19) You're Making Your Financial Adviser Rich
www.bloombergview.com/articles/2016-04-11/those-tiny-fees-make-your-financial-adviser-rich
taken 12 April 2016

(20) HOG Form 10-K Quarterly SEC Filing
investor.harley-davidson.com/phoenix.zhtml?c=87981&p=irol-reportsannual
taken 13 April 2016

(21) The Millionaire Real Estate Investor
www.amazon.com/The-Millionaire-Real-Estate-Investor/dp/0071446370
taken 22 April 2016

(22) Funding fee tables
www.benefits.va.gov/homeloans/documents/docs/funding_fee_table.pdf
taken 26 April 2016

(23) Retirement savings contributions credit (saver's credit)
www.irs.gov/Retirement-Plans/Plan-Participant,-Employee/Retirement-Savings-Contributions-Savers-Credit
taken 3 May 2016

(24) More Millionaires than ever are living in the US
www.cnbc.com/2015/03/09/more-millionaires-than-ever-are-living-in-the-us.html
taken 25 June 2016

ABOUT THE AUTHOR

Chris Lehto has been an F-16 pilot since 2002 and instructs new F-16 pilots. He has a Bachelor's of Science in Chemistry-Materials Science from the Air Force Academy and a Masters in Aeronautical Science from Embry Riddle University. He has been stationed in South Korea, Italy, Alaska, Turkey and several locations in the contiguous US. His background and training allow him to provide a new and unique viewpoint to the fitness and finance worlds. He grew up in Houston and currently lives with his wife and three little kids in Arizona.

www.ingramcontent.com/pod-product-compliance
Lightning Source LLC
Chambersburg PA
CBHW060353190526
45169CB00002B/586